FIRST BOOK OF CREATIVE RHYTHMS

FIRST BOOK OF

MUSIC

Eleanor Farjeon

Can you dance?
I love to dance!
Music is my happy chance.
Music playing
In the street
Gets into
My hands and feet. . . .

Can you play?
I love to play!
Practice music everyday
Then you'll give
The world a chance
To dance and sing,
To sing and dance.

CREATIVE RHYTHMS

Rosanna B. Saffran

Special Teacher of Instrumental Music
Music Department, Elementary Schools, Washington, D.C.

HOLT, RINEHART and WINSTON, INC.
New York   Chicago   San Francisco   Toronto   London

23340

CONTENTS

PREFACE

The decision to write a book on early rhythmic activities stems from the need for such a book expressed by the author's co-workers in two cities (Philadelphia and Washington, D.C.). These kindergarten and primary grade teachers have recognized the importance and value of rhythmic activities for children. They have also indicated the following areas of uncertainty in presenting rhythms in the classroom: (1) an insecurity about teaching music in general; (2) an inability to play the piano (they recognize that phonograph records and songs cannot do the whole job); (3) an unsureness about how and where to begin developing true creativity in an organized manner. It is the aim of this book to deal with these problems and to help teachers give systematic direction to creative activities in the classroom.

The busy life of the teacher and the minor role assigned to rhythms in the primary curriculum necessitate the writing of a concise and practical book. Piano music has been selected to suit the elementary player. While effort has been expended to keep the music close to the original, it has been necessary to make adaptations. For the most part, the musical selections are passages freely extracted from larger compositions. Transposition, rhythmic alteration, simplified notation, and changes in tempo and dynamics occur when justified by considerations of practicality and usefulness in the classroom situation. Means of using rhythm instruments are described for the nonpianist. Although enough material is included to make the book self-sufficient, supplementary material is listed for those who may desire it.

The educational importance and values of creative rhythms in the classroom are briefly discussed in Chapter 1. It is assumed that the teacher has "learned her lessons" and now wants practical materials rather than a mere theoretical

A word of advice to the teacher: Teach rhythmic activities because you want to, not because you have to. You will then have fun with your children, and you will grow musically with them.

ACKNOWLEDGMENTS

The author wishes to express appreciation to the following people for their invaluable assistance in the preparation of this book: William E. Hess, Philadelphia, Pennsylvania; Sara L. Hughes, Washington, D.C.; the author's associates in the Washington, D.C., Public Schools; Laura Pendleton McCarteney; the librarians of the Education Library, University of Michigan; Martha J. Baldwin; and the author's husband, Herman E. Saffran.

Washington, D.C.   R. B. S.

1

INTRODUCTION

Some Questions and Answers

1. What are rhythms?

    In this book, rhythms are defined as physical responses to sound.

2. What values do rhythms have for children in the classroom?

    They help develop five major educational objectives:
    Active listening habits.
    Independent thought.
    Language ability and concepts.
    Muscular growth and coordination.
    Musical insights.

    There are many other values:
    Initiative is easily stimulated.
    Each child attains a measure of success.
    Shy children lose their inhibitions.
    Aggressive children are given an outlet for pent-up energies while at the same time learning control.
    All children achieve a certain degree of self-discovery.
    Rhythms are an excellent means of relaxation and enjoyment.

3. Do the benefits derived from rhythms belong only to the music phase of the curriculum?

    Emphatically, no! Here are other areas of the curriculum that benefit:
    Language arts. Vocabulary is increased through the use of emotional words (sad, happy, gay, depressed); descriptive words (swaying, twisting, waddling, bending); comparative words (tall, short, low, high); words of intensity (quiet, noisy, loud, soft).

    Reading readiness is developed through increased concepts, discrimination, and perception.

1

Enjoyment of literature and poetry is augmented by rhythmic interpretation.

Social studies. Rhythms express or dramatize activities in the home (sewing, rocking baby, mowing lawn); transportation (trains, planes); animals (waddling ducks, swaying elephants); community helpers (hammering carpenter, telephone lineman).

Science. Rhythms help children to become aware of sounds (breaking waves, storm) and to perceive the world around them (swaying leaves, moving wheels, growing plants, shooting rockets).

Arithmetic. The rhythms lesson helps children to count by finding out how many children will perform at a time, by discovering how many chairs will be needed, by counting beats in the measure while moving, by counting steps, jumps, hops, and the like in developing movement patterns.

Music. Rhythms help develop an awareness and insight into meter, rhythm, and structure.

The children will come to associate good music with enjoyment.

4. What standard methods of approach are used to develop rhythmic activities?

The *formal* (or *patterned*) *method*. The teacher determines the detailed movements that the children are expected to follow strictly.

The *informal method*. A verbal accompaniment is provided. Its content determines the children's movements, and they can interpret freely within that context. This method employs:

Mimetics—everyday actions such as hammering, sweeping.
Impersonation—"Let's pretend we are airplanes, giants."
Dramatization—acting with poetry, songs, action records.
Singing games—"Farmer in the Dell," and others.

The *creative method*. The children are encouraged physically to express feelings derived from music (usually a recording). Responses depend solely upon the child's own past experiences; no bodily movements are suggested or taught.

The Modified Rhythmic Approach

The modified rhythmic approach described in this book has been used in classrooms for some years, and has been proved effective in stimulating truly creative rhythms. As defined here, creative rhythms are *original physical responses to sound, derived from experiences based upon a systematic foundation.* Such a groundwork is necessary for any creative endeavor. By providing an organized foundation, the modified rhythmic approach is designed to achieve a full realization of creative rhythms.

This approach has been developed for teachers who, as the school year progresses, often find disturbing problems developing that lead them to a distaste for the creative rhythms period. Some of these problems are a loss of genuine interest and enjoyment by the children; a retrogression in their ability to interpret the music, or very little development after the initial stages; and an inability for the children to respond to music without additional prompting. The class settles down to a few limited responses done in a routine manner. In the final evaluation of the program, the teacher finds that no real creativity has been achieved.

After many years of observing and experimenting in classrooms, it has been found that these problems stem from the approach utilized, not from the teacher's lack of musical ability or the children's lack of intellect.

The three standard approaches are described in the questions and answers above. Each is of some value and the use of any one is better than giving no rhythmic experience at all. But none of these approaches by itself can develop insight and feeling for true and varied creative movements.

The formal (or patterned) method when used by itself cannot lead to creativity. Nothing is wrong with the movements called for, but with the manner in which they are obtained. When children are required to be in exact step and to move in a quiet, orderly line or circle, they are being forced to respond like automatons.

With little opportunity to think, children will fail to progress in interpretive ability.

On the other hand, the informal method leads young children to a dependence upon suggestions or cues, without allowing them to derive the rhythm from the music. Here, too, the class thinking is done for them, and they lose their ability to respond without a crutch.

The creative method, also described, is not employed in the modified rhythmic approach. Certainly creative response is the goal, but a child's experience is not wide enough to provide all the raw material for reaching that goal. Beginning with the end product, as is done in the creative method, results in limited, stereotyped responses and lagging interest.

The modified rhythmic approach employs elements of both the formal method and informal method in combination. The natural body movements of the formal method are used alone or in combination with useful suggestions involving mimetics and impersonation. The children are trained to listen critically to musical rhythm, pitch, and tempo. The music (or rhythmic accompaniment) determines the physical response. Words are used only for motivation or evaluation; they are not used as directions during the actual responses. The children gain an ability freely to interpret rhythms with natural body actions discovered by means of motivation and experimentation. They learn that the same music (or rhythmic accompaniment) can imply different physical movements.

Rhythms do not become monotonous when there is an element of discovery in new movements, combinations, or variations in movements. Action songs, records, and singing games do not become routine; rather they have their place in the program as special treats, once true rhythmic feeling is generated.

The teacher should refrain from influencing the children's interpretive movements; for they are interpretive, right from the start. It is important for children to feel rhythms and respond naturally with their bodies. Their muscular control and coordination of movement are still in a developmental stage. During this stage, the teacher is a wise guide—not a director. For example, the teacher should discard preconceived adult notions of how a tiger slinks or how an airplane flies. It is not desirable to set adult standards of interpretation. Rather, the teacher should help establish a groundwork of rhythmic responses and then merely guide the children as they participate in creative rhythms.

2

HOW TO USE
THIS BOOK

The purpose of this book is to present briefly and simply a systematic method of developing natural body responses. The foundation for creative responses is based upon the accumulated knowledge of the basic steps and their variations, as well as the manner in which they are developed.

Many teachers feel that piano playing ability and musicianship are essential; this book should prove otherwise. It is written so that those who feel uncertainty need only closely follow the text to gain the desired results. Piano accompaniments are provided to add interest to the program, but their use is not mandatory. In fact, even the accomplished pianist should use the other rhythmic devices suggested. Supplementary materials are listed for those desiring additional sources. If the teacher prefers to use her own musical selections, the given rhythmic patterns and music will guide her choices.

Format of the Rhythms Chapters

Following the introductory chapters, the main body of the text is devoted to a series of chapters, one for each basic rhythmic movement. For purposes of unity, all chapters on foot movements are grouped together, followed by the chapters on body movements. The order of presentation of the steps need not be that given in the book. For example, body movements can be introduced much earlier than they appear, and thereafter, foot and body movements can be interspersed.

Each chapter contains a description of the step (if necessary), suggestions for motivation, rhythm instruments to be used in place of or in conjunction with the piano, an outline of the rhythmic beat (for use with the rhythm instruments), piano accompaniments, variations in the basic step, lists of poetry and supplementary music source materials, and (sometimes) useful reminders. The elements of the rhythms lesson are discussed more fully below.

Motivation

When introducing a rhythm to your class, be brief. At the beginning, follow the technique described in Chapter 4. Later, a sentence or two of introduction, a poem, or a very short discussion is usually sufficient. Sometimes prior motivation is not needed, but discussion or evaluation should be used after the initial rhythmic response to improve the children's understanding of the rhythm. In this case too, brevity is important. Long discussions are frustrating to children who want to move.

The use of poetry is often very effective in motivating rhythms. A poem may directly or indirectly suggest a particular action, or it may merely set a mood. Poems that clearly describe an action usually need to be followed only by a single statement such as "How do you think the horse galloped?" Poems that are more indirect in content will also produce excellent results if they are preceded or followed by a short discussion channeled in the desired direction. Children have much imagination. Give them a chance to use it!

Remember that in rhythms, poetry is used for motivation only. It should not become a basis for dramatization. Never read poetry while the children are moving. The children should not imitate the action of a poem, but rather should use some idea or some mood suggested by the poem as a basis for elaborating on their own ideas. If Mary thinks she is best conveying the sluggishness of the elephant while remaining upright, who is to say otherwise?

Introduction of Basic Steps

When a new basic step is introduced, always use it in its natural form only; that is, walking is to be done in the children's individual speeds and patterns. Do not attempt to have them conform to a set speed or mode of walking, but pace your accompaniment to their own. Each child will begin to sense the rhythm and tempo of his walk. Next the group will become aware of and will adjust to each other's rhythms and tempos and then, gradually and effortlessly, they will respond to the given rhythms and tempos.

Here are some suggestions that involve a minimum of time and effort, and have always been proved successful. In the initial rhythms lesson period, which should be a part of the first school day, the teacher herself should participate in the motions. Her example will set the area of movement and direction (see Chapter 4). When she stops chanting to the step, her movement stops too, and all the children should follow. If some continue moving, the class needs to be told that "The music (or the accompaniment) tells us what to do. We stop when it stops." Such reminders must be repeated intermittently during the first few weeks; after that only an occasional "The music stopped" should be necessary.

During the first lesson, either basic walking alone or walking and running (both basic) can be used. This is a matter for the teacher to decide.

Variations in the Steps

To achieve the desired goal of creativity, the children must first be made conscious of the basic steps they are using, such as walking, running. Then, as a continual process, they must be awakened to the many variations they can produce through natural body movements. They should be constantly helped to recognize differences in dynamics such as loud and soft, differences in tempo such as fast and slow, differences in mood such as happy and sad, differences in motion such as smooth and jerky. With continual motivation and evaluation, children will become aware of the fact that feet or arms can be used alone or in combination, that when they are moving up and down or sidewards, they are moving in space, and that through exploration, they can find many different ways of performing a basic step, thus creating new steps and patterns.

The accompaniment, too, helps in stimulating more ideas for variation. The same percussive instrument played a little differently (a change in tempo or dynamics or accent) produces a different physical response.

Let the children learn to create by discovering for themselves the variations and ways of combining them. Here is one of the best opportunities for developing attention span, critical listening, insight, language ability, and vocabulary.

Combinations

Combining the rhythms is merely putting together what has come before. Once a rhythm is used, it can become a part of any rhythms lesson. As new steps are learned, they are combined with those previously learned.

Examples:
1. Basic walk—basic run—basic walk . . . .
2. Basic walk—tiptoe walk—basic walk—fast run—slow walk . . . .
3. Basic walk—tiptoe walk—fast walk—lumbering walk . . . .
4. Fast run—basic walk—fast run—basic march—basic walk . . . .
5. Heavy walk—basic jump—slow march—fast run—limping walk . . . .

The number of ways to combine the rhythms is limited only by the imagination of the accompanist (whether teacher or child). The length of time or number of measures for each step can be varied; use four, eight, twelve, or sixteen measures for each step, and alternate the steps between fast and slow or between quiet and active movements. This is not only for variety and to maintain alertness, but also to prevent the children from becoming tired or overly stimulated. By the middle of the school year the combination would follow a pattern such as this: walking—jumping—swaying—marching—galloping—sliding—running.

The accompaniments for these rhythm combinations are played continuously. Changes in rhythm are introduced without pause—in the spirit of a game without words, just rhythmic sounds. Although some advance warning of such changes is necessary in the beginning, it should be omitted as soon as possible. (See Chapter 4 for techniques of introducing combinations; see also Chapter 19.)

If this procedure is used in the early stages and in the manner suggested, observe how quickly and easily the children develop independence of response to rhythmic sounds without the need for words or titles to suggest action. And with this, observe a growing ability for critical thinking and an increasing discriminatory power.

Accompaniments

All of the music in this book has been selected for its musical value. It is fairly easy and is satisfactory when played with the right hand alone. Thus, an elementary player should require very little practice. The Index of Piano Music lists all the piano music available in this book.

In addition, various rhythm instruments and other means for accompaniment are suggested. Use several types of accompaniment, either one at a time or in combination.

If rhythm instruments are not available, they are easily made, and their construction presents an opportunity for a meaningful project. In addition, rhythmic accompaniments can be produced by rapping pencils or dowel pins on the desk or floor or against each other, by clapping hands, or tapping feet.

Teachers without playing ability can also use the piano. For example, a lumbering walk can be accompanied by playing two low keys alternately in a slow even rhythm; running or tumbling by fast runs of three or four notes; jumping and hopping by a series of chords staccato; bending and stretching by alternating a middle key and a high key. All of the above can be done with one hand. In like fashion, one should experiment with the rhythm instruments. Note the changing pitch produced by using different surfaces, or by using different beaters.

The teacher should also make much use of the rhythms given in the outline of the rhythmic beats for each step. An Index of Basic Rhythmic Patterns is given at the end of the book.

Rhythm records and action records have their place in a well-rounded music program; however, they do not lend themselves to the early procedure with its need for fitting the accompaniment to the children's speed. Even later they afford little opportunity for original response unless they contain only music without words. In any event, they should never be identified to the children as "marching music" and the like.

Action records do have some value in teaching the children to listen and follow directions and are best used as supplementary materials late in the year. They are especially appreciated when presented as an occasional treat. Too early and too exclusive use of recordings tends to encourage dull, automatic response and a dependence upon words for action.

Supplementary Materials

As stated earlier, the methods and means of accompaniment suggested in this book should be sufficient to meet a teacher's needs. However, for those who desire them, the titles of additional piano music for given rhythms are supplied at the end of each chapter. So also are poems that can be used for motivation. These lists have been taken from sources usually available to the classroom. For further information, a bibliography of publications in this field is given at the end of the book.

3

RHYTHMS
IN THE CLASSROOM:
Some Problems
and Solutions

Space

Space is a common problem, but not an insurmountable one.

If there is an open area in the front, rear or at the sides or middle of the classroom, use it. It will limit only the number of participants at a given time.

No open area? Stationary furniture? Use the aisles or fringes of the room. Limit the number of children moving.

Movable furniture was put into classrooms for just such activities. To avoid hubbub and disorder when creating space and putting the room back in order again, plan a simple moving procedure, or have the children help make the plan. Devise a method for releasing the most space by moving the least amount of furniture. Usually, just a few tables or desks pushed back or to the side will do the job.

For the first month or so, continue to give specific directions and help with the moving. When the procedure becomes routine and rapid, it can become part of the daily (or weekly) helpers' plan. Be sure a planned procedure is followed for replacing furniture into position for the next activity.

The outdoor play area is a wonderful place for teaching rhythms, even when there is classroom space. The all-purpose room and auditorium should not be overlooked as good places for rhythmic activities, too.

Time

The amount of time spent for the rhythms presentation will vary with the time of the year. In September, five minutes is often sufficient and by June, fifteen minutes. Sometimes there may be several periods in the day for rhythms, as during dramatic play. Children playing trains may find their pretending furthered by using a simple sand block. Playing horses can be enhanced by a galloping rhythm on a wood block.

The amount of time needed for trying or creating a new step or variation usually is a minute or two, but its development takes the whole year.

Number of Children

Because beginner's shyness is universal in young children, it is best to start with everyone moving. If space is limited, take the class outdoors so that there is room for all to move freely. Starting rhythms activities with the group moving as a whole does much to prevent later problems of reticence and insecurity. After several weeks, the class can be divided in half. The group sitting on the sidelines can clap hands or tap rhythm instruments, using either measured beats or the actual rhythm.

Directions or Rules

There are two rules, or patterns, that the teacher must set during the first lesson:
1. The children must be guided to try to do what the music tells them.
2. The direction in which they are to move must be established so that they will not bump into each other.

Directions or demonstrations on how to walk, run, swing, and so forth, should be rare. If the music or rhythm is well-defined and set to the children's speed, there will be very few who cannot keep in step. Commands for group conformity are unnecessary restrictions that will dampen enthusiasm and hamper the development of natural responses.

Organization

An avoidance of rules regarding the rhythmic steps does not mean that disorganization must occur. A few simple directions for procedure are essential to maintain an orderly activity and, given in an incidental manner, are accepted and followed without detriment to the activity.

Thus, defining the area of movement, planning the shifting of furniture, deciding the direction of motion, insuring that stopping occurs when the accompaniment stops, and advocating moving at the same tempo as the music are the essential steps toward an organization that avoids problems.

Props

The use of flags, ribbons, scarves, balloons, hoops, also adds interest and variety to the rhythms lesson. It is suggested that only one prop be used at a time and that their use be introduced only after the children have gained confidence in their movements.

Behavior Problems

With a few restrictions, good organization, continued motivation and challenge, plus the teacher's recognition that seeming nonconformity may be honest experimentation with motion, misbehavior and rowdyism will be rare.

Rapid movements such as running and galloping can excite some of the children to race. When this happens, help the children understand that the accompaniment is telling them how fast to go, or that some children are going faster than the music is telling them. Remind the children to listen more carefully.

Well-planned rhythmic activities often help the aggressive child by providing a useful outlet for his excess energy.

The retiring child is drawn in when he sees other children participating. If no difficult demands are made upon him, he will usually take part happily. The unrestricted movement helps him gain self-confidence because he can perform satisfactorily, and there is no need for vocal response. When he is chosen to be a partner, the casual nature of the activity called for is quite apt to make him forget his reticence.

If behavior problems do occur in rhythms class, the teacher should look first into her own role in the lesson. Perhaps the children have had insufficient motivation or challenge, or perhaps they do not comprehend; they might need some further suggestion as a stimulus, or might be getting tired of the activity; maybe there has been too much sameness, or the period has been too long.

In most cases, when behavior problems develop during rhythms, it is time for a change. Depending upon the situation, either terminate the lesson, try some new motivation, discuss ways to vary the movement, change to a completely contrasting type of rhythm, discuss the problem, or have a little quiet music "to put the baby to sleep."

WALKING
Grace Ellen Glaubitz

When Daddy
Walks
With Jean and me,
We have a
Lot of fun
'Cause we can't
Walk as fast
As he,
Unless we
Skip and
Run!
I stretch,
And stretch
My legs so far,
I nearly slip
And fall—
But how
Does Daddy
Take such steps?
He doesn't stretch
At all!

4

WALKING

Basic Walking

Motivation: Use action immediately. Start the entire group walking informally.
1. Say, "Let's take a walk around the room."
   Take two children by the hand. Start walking, and tell the others to follow.
2. When the children have set a tempo, chant a word accompaniment to the tempo, such as "Let's take a walk, walk, walk around the room." Continue this for a minute or two; then stop.
3. Suggest taking a walk to somewhere, like the store, school, or to visit a friend, and repeat steps 1 and 2, changing the words to fit the destination.
4. Release the hands of the children, and join their hands. Say, "I am going to clap the way you are walking. Go."
5. Repeat, changing the destination of the walk and the type of accompaniment.
6. "Now, I am going to play some music. Listen carefully. Then when I say go, see if you can walk the way the music tells you. Listen." Play two or four measures as introduction, then, without stopping, say, "Go."

Accompaniments: Clap hands, tap stick or sticks, glasses, wood blocks, large drum, autoharp, piano.

Rhythmic beat: Even and steady.

Count 1 2 3 4   1 2 3 4   1 2 3   1 2 3   1,2 3,4 1,2 3,4

Reminders:
1. Stop the activity when the music stops. (See Chapter 2, under the heading "Introduction of Basic Steps.")
2. Always play accompaniments at the tempo set by the children.
3. In the early lessons, do not stop the children if they join in the chanting or continue chanting with the accompaniment.
4. When movement stops, commend the children's awareness.
5. Most children are timid at the beginning; thus the teacher suggests the movement and takes part. This helps the children relax and restrains the more vociferous child from talking too much.

Variations in Walking

Variations in tempo and dynamics: Fast, slow; soft, loud; short, long; heavy, light.

Variations in mood: Happy, sad, jaunty, pensive, angry.

Variations in foot movements: On heels, shuffling, toes in or out, on outside of feet, peg leg.

Variations in direction: Forward, backward, sideward, circle, zigzag.

Motivation: Associate the actions with some current phase of class interest or with familiar sounds, objects, or people.

Examples:

1. When discussing the family, read the poem "Walking." Ask the children if they can show how their fathers walk. Ask if they can walk like their mothers, and so through the family.
2. To elicit from the children different types of tip-toe movements, discuss Halloween goblins. How do they travel about? Do they move fast or slow, loud or soft? Let the children demonstrate. Ask them to analyze their foot movements.
3. Other topics to aid in developing variations are animals, elves, walking in snow, walking to church with the family, strolling through the park, going on errands, having a sore foot.

Reminders:

1. Always try to stimulate the imagination of the children so the variations will be theirs alone.
2. Avoid demonstrating or teaching a step.
3. Be alert to the children's comments and movements. Their natural responses are better than adult ones.
4. Discovered new steps or patterns should be given their descriptive terms as peg leg, zigzag, jaunty.
5. For additional walking music in this book, see the Index of Piano Music.

Suggested Poetry for Motivation

(*Numbers following the listed poems are keyed to the Poetry References at the back of the book*)

Bacmeister, R., "Galoshes" (or "Susie's Galoshes")[1, 3, 12]
Brisley, J. L., "Which?"[4]
Farjeon, E., "Mrs. Peck-Pigeon"[1, 2]
Lindsay, V., "The Mysterious Cat" (Stanzas 1 and 5)[1, 5, 6]
Milne, A. A., "Puppy and I"[1, 7]
Willson, D., "Tip-Toe Tale"[4]
Wylie, E., "Velvet Shoes"[1, 5]
Wynne, A., "The Elephant"[4]

BOURRÉE

(BASIC WALK)

Georg Philipp Telemann

GERMAN DANCE NO. 6
from "Seven German Dances"

(TIPTOE WALK)

Franz Joseph Haydn

AIR

(STATELY WALK)

Henry Purcell

Moderately slowly

FOR CHILDREN
Vol. I, No. XI

(LUMBERING WALK)

Béla Bartók

Very slowly

WALKING

18

THE BEAR

(LUMBERING WALK)

Vladimir Rebikov

Slowly

SUNDAY MORNING
Op. 96, No. 1

Albert Löschhorn

(LUMBERING WALK)

Slowly

WALKING

19

Supplementary Music for Accompaniment

(Numbers following the listed music are keyed to the Music References at the back of the book)

The American Singer, Book One[1]
> Grieg, E., "Hall of the Mountain King" (p. 121)
> Haydn, F. J., "Theme" (p. 114)
> Reinhold, H., "Gypsy Song" (p. 118)

Music for Young Americans, Kindergarten Book[2]
> Elston, R., "Theme" (p. 98)
> Hooley, D., "Happy Days" (p. 100)
> Pace, R., "Promenade" (p. 99)
> Schumann, R., "Little Piece" (p. 109)
> Waite, F., "Chorale" (p. 98)

Music for Young Americans, Book One[3]
> Mitchell, L., "Promenade" (p. 115)
> Pace, R., "Indian Dance" (p. 131)
> Tchaikovsky, P. I., "Chorale" (p. 116)

Birchard Music Series, Book One[4]
> Bartok, B., "Children At Play" (p. 170)
> Bartok, B., "Play" (p. 148)
> English Folk Song, "Bells" (p. 146)
> Gretchaninov, A., "Morning Walk" (p. 153)
> Kabalevsky, D., "A Game" (p. 173)
> Kabalevsky, D., "Polka" (p. 156)
> Liadov, A., "The Music Box" (p. 171)
> Old French Tune, "Bourrée" (p. 150)
> Schumann, R., "Humming Song" (p. 133)
> Zhilinsky, "Latvian Song" (p. 156)

Birchard Music Series, Kindergarten Book[5]
> Gluck, C., "Musette" (p. 143)
> Tansman, A., "Bouncing Ball" (p. 142)

Music for Early Childhood[6]
> Still, W. G., "Bear" (p. 50)
> Still, W. G., "Camel" (p. 49)
> Still, W. G., "Elephant" (p. 53)

Experiences in Music for First Grade Children[7]
> Reinhold, H., "Lightly Stepping" (p. 13)

Music through the Day, Teacher's Book[8]
> Gretchaninoff, A., "Out for a Walk" (p. 131)
> Hebrides Folk Tune, "Going to Pasture" (p. 63)
> Hollaender, A., "March" (p. 139)
> Rameau, J. P., "Tambourin" (p. 151)

Our Singing World, The Kindergarten Book[9]
> Anderson, C. L., "Walking in the Snow" (p. 101)
> Ghys, H., "Amaryllis" (p. 21)
> Gluck, C. W., "Dance of the Happy Spirits" (p. 34)

Gretchaninoff, A., "The Little Traveller" (p. 24)
Gurlitt, C., "Let's Take a Walk" (p. 23)
Hollaender, A., "March" (p. 121)
Jadassohn, S., "Air de Ballet" (p. 24)
Reinhold, H., "Nocturne" (p. 74)
Our Singing World, The First Grade Book[10]
Anderson, C. L., "Walking in the Rain" (p. 126)
Balfe, M. W., "A Soldier's Life" (p. 38)
Delibes, L, "Passepied" (p. 134)
Kullak, T., "The Clock" (p. 164)
Swiss Folk Tune, "The Swiss Maid" (p. 15)
Tchaikovsky, P. I., "The Doll's Burial" (p. 169)
This Is Music, Book One[11]
Traditional English Dance, "The Staines Morris Tune" (p. 184)

RUNNING
Kate Greenaway

What is Tommy running for
    Running for
    Running for?
What is Tommy running for,
    On this fine day?

Jimmy will run after Tommy,
    After Tommy,
    After Tommy,
That's what Tommy's running for
    On this fine day.

Poem reprinted from *Marigold Garden/Under the Window* by Kate Greenaway with the permission of the publishers, Frederick Warne & Company.

5

RUNNING

Basic Running

Motivation:
1. "Mother sends you to the store to buy some butter. It is a very hot day. She says, 'Hurry back or the butter will melt.' Show me how you will go back home with the butter."
2. As the children move, run with them and chant to their speed. "Run, run, run, run!" or "Hurry, hurry!"
3. When they have gotten the butter home, comment on the action. "That was fine, but I see some butter dripping. I think some of you didn't go fast enough. Try it again. Go!" Use a rhythm instrument for accompaniment.
4. Repeat, changing the reason for running, and using a new accompaniment.
5. Continue in a manner similar to that in step 6 in the example under the heading "Basic Walking" in Chapter 4.

Accompaniments: Rhythm sticks, triangle, rattle, tambourine, small drum, autoharp, piano.

Rhythmic beat: Rapid and even.

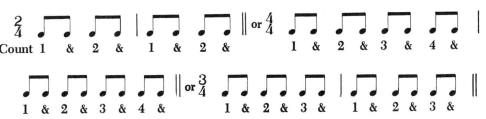

Reminders:
1. When a step is first introduced, use only the basic (natural) form.
2. Be brief in giving motivation and directions.
3. Do not talk or comment while the children are in motion.
4. Accompaniment should follow the speed set by children.
5. In deference to the shy child, avoid asking questions requiring oral answers during the first week or two.

Variations in Running

Variations in tempo and dynamics: Fast, slow; soft, loud; short, long; heavy, light.

Variations in mood: Happy, playful, hurrying.

Variations in direction: Circle, zigzag, forward, backward, sideward, combinations of these to form patterns.

Motivation:

1. After the children have been walking like members of the family (see Chapter 4), continue with:
    "You just walked like your father walks. Can you run like he does? What kind of steps does he take, big or little? Do his steps sound loud or soft? Show me."
2. Or, "We left two chairs in the middle of the room. How many ways can you find to run around the two chairs without bumping into each other?" Let the children describe the patterns they used (zigzag, circles around individual chairs).
3. Or, "Let's be birds, airplanes, train wheels, patter of rain, kittens." (Select appropriate poetry for motivation.)

Reminders:

1. Motivation is used only for developing new movements, either basic steps or variations.
2. When repeating a familiar rhythmic movement, play a few measures of the accompaniment while the children listen carefully to see what the music is telling them to do. Then, repeat from the beginning while they respond.

Suggested Poetry for Motivation

(See Poetry References)
Aldis, D., "Ice"[1, 2, 3, 4, 12]
Baruch, D., "Different Bicycles"[1]
Baruch, D., "Merry-Go-Round"[1, 3, 5, 11]
Follen, E., "Runaway Brook"[4]
Green, M. McB., "Aeroplane"[1, 3]
Tippett, J. S., "Trains"[1, 2, 4, 13]

LES TAMBOURINS

Johann Philipp Kirnberger

Moderately fast

TAMBOURIN

Louis-Claude Daquin

Fast

THE DANCING MASTER

Daniel Gottlob Türk

(TIPTOE RUN)

Moderately fast

RUNNING

25

SCHERZO
from Sonatina No. 4

Franz Joseph Haydn

Supplementary Music for Accompaniment

(*See Music References*)
The American Singer, Book One[1]
    Grieg, E., "Hall of the Mountain King" (p. 121)
    Gurlitt, C., "The Fair" (p. 117)
Music for Young Americans, Kindergarten Book[2]
    Hooley, D., "Little Study" (p. 99)
    Kabalevsky, D., "A Fairy Tale" (p. 108)
Music for Young Americans, Book One[3]
    Pace, R., "On the Move" (p. 117)
    Riccio, M., "Starlight" (p. 118)
Birchard Music Series, Book One[4]
    Kabalevsky, D., "Running Along" (p. 160)
    Russian Folk Song, "Pretty Minka" (p. 159)
Birchard Music Series, Kindergarten Book[5]
    Danish Folk Dance, "Crested Hen" (p. 139)
    Tcherepnin, A., "Relays" (p. 152)
Music for Early Childhood[6]
    Still, W. G., "Lamb" (p. 52)
Experiences in Music for First Grade Children[7]
    Mueller, E. A., "The Brook" (p. 131)
    Vene, R., "Catch My Doggie" (p. 14)

RUNNING

Music through the Day, Teacher's Book[8]
    Couperin, F., "The Little Windmills" (p. 156)
    Delibes, L., "Passepied" (p. 158)
    Grieg, E., "Puck" (p. 145)
    Kabalevsky, D., "A Little Joke" (p. 138)
Our Singing World, Kindergarten Book[9]
    Concone, G., "Run, Run, Run!" (p. 11)
    Gurlitt, C., "Running Game" (p. 12)
Our Singing World, The First Grade Book[10]
    Heller, S., "Petite Tarantelle" (p. 33)
    Kullak, T., "The Clock" (p. 164)
    Mendelssohn, F., "Planes and Trains" (p. 193)
    Planquette, R., "Running" (p. 13)
    Schumann, R., "The Little Breeze" (p. 122)
    Swiss Folk Tune, "The Swiss Maid" (p. 15)
This Is Music, Book One[11]
    Russian Folk Tune, "Kamarinskaia" (p. 184)

WHICH WAY?
Lois Atkinson

Poor Wendy Whichaway never really knew
Exactly the way to go for what she had to do.
She once ran when she started
On a three-mile hike.
She then ran up a mountain
While she pushed along her bike.
She walked like molasses
When she was "it" at tag.
She walked to school when she was late
And made her teacher nag.
She walked when it was icy cold.
She ran when it was hot.
Wherever Wendy started to
Was where she never got.

6

WALKING AND RUNNING

Basic Walking and Running Combined

When most of the children demonstrate an ability to follow given rhythms for walking and running, it is time to begin combinations of these two steps. This procedure initiates the cumulative process in which each movement is added to those previously learned. As a result, the habit of careful listening starts and the ability to discriminate grows. In the very early stages, there is little need for suggestion; instead, a recognition of rhythmic sounds is the criterion for action. So begins creative response.

Motivation:
1. Review walking and running in a manner similar to the original presentation. You set the speed.
2. Then say, "I'm going to play. The music (or the sound) will tell you what to do. See if you can hear whether it tells you to walk or run. Listen. What did it tell you to do? That's correct, walk. Now you walk the way it tells you." Repeat the music.
3. Say, "I'm going to play again. Do what the music tells you to do this time. Listen." Repeat walking using another form of accompaniment. Some will answer, "Run." Tell these children to try it with the accompaniment and then decide. Now repeat walking for the whole class.
4. Follow steps 2 and 3 for running.
5. Inform the children that the music will change rhythm without stopping. "Listen carefully or you may be fooled." Play eight measures each of walking and running rhythms. Alternate these two rhythms several times.
6. Finally, make a game of the combinations. Tease them: vary the lengths of time for each step, continue without pause between steps, or briefly pause at unexpected times and repeat the step. Do not tell the children of the changes in advance. You may need to use a simple reminder: "Listen carefully, or you may be fooled."

Accompaniments: Large and small drums, or any combination of instruments suggested under walking and running.

Rhythmic beat:

Reminders:
1. Hereafter, walking and running in combined form (varying the order without a pause or a reminder to the children when changing rhythms) should become a standard part of each rhythms period.
2. If the piano is used, any piece of music under walking or running may be used for either. Use a slow to moderate tempo for walking and a faster tempo for running.
3. If the piano is not used, use the Basic Rhythmic Patterns Index at the back of the book for walking and running. Follow a similar procedure whenever adding new steps to a combination.

Variations in the Walking and Running Combination

After combinations of basic steps are established, review a variation of walking and one of running, and then combine them as described in Motivation steps 2 to 6 at the beginning of this chapter. When this has been accomplished, combine basic walking, basic running, and one variation of each in the following manner:

"Children, we're going to play our game again. Sometimes the music will tell us to walk tiptoe; sometimes it will tell us just to walk; sometimes to run tiptoe, or to run fast. Listen carefully, I'm going to try to fool you." Play eight measures each of basic walking, of the variation in walking, of basic running, and of the variation in running. Repeat, changing the order of the steps. Continue with the game, pausing unexpectedly, varying the number of measures used for each step, and so forth.

Format of the Rhythms Lesson: From this point on, the three procedures below are to be used in any order.
1. A combination of the familiar basic steps and variations.
2. Learning a new basic step and/or drawing forth the discovery of a new variation or variations.
3. The addition of another basic step to the combination as soon as the children have become secure in that step.

WALKING AND RUNNING
30

Examples:
1. Basic walking and running used with one or two variations that have been

developed. These steps are then used in several combinations such as walking with variations, running with variations, or walking and running with variations.

2. In the next lesson, repeat these combinations, and also find new variations on walking or running. During this lesson also introduce the next basic step—marching.

3. Repeat the above during the next lesson or two, at the same time introducing variations in marching.

4. When the children seem familiar with the marching rhythm, use a combined form of walking, running, and marching. In the same lesson, introduce basic jumping.

5. Repeat the above in another lesson period, using variations in the combined form of walking, running, and marching. In this same period, introduce variations in jumping.

6. When children respond well with jumping rhythms, add them to the combinations.

Reminders:

1. Permit freedom of action. Do not stop a child from varying his step even though it does not fit your preconceived plan.

2. Although the teacher sets the tempo in combinations, it should be close to the children's speed.

3. For further discussion of combinations see Chapters 2 and 19.

GAVOTTE AND VARIATION

Johann Pachelbel

PART I (BASIC WALK)

Moderately

PART II (BASIC RUN)

Moderately

GAVOTTE AND VARIATION (Continued)

PART III (STATELY WALK)

PART IV (HIGH-STEPPING RUN)

GAVOTTE AND VARIATION

PART I (BASIC WALK)

George Frederick Handel

Moderately

PART II (TIPTOE WALK; REPEAT PART I, PLAY A LITTLE SLOWER, SOFTLY AND LIGHTLY, AS BELOW)

Moderately slowly

**WALKING
AND
RUNNING**

GAVOTTE AND VARIATION (Continued)

PART III (BASIC RUN)

PART IV (HEAVY RUN; REPEAT PART III, PLAY A LITTLE SLOWER, WITH MARKED ACCENTS, AS BELOW)

WALKING
AND
RUNNING
35

CHILDREN'S BALLET

Daniel Gottlob Türk

PART I (BASIC WALK)

Moderately

PART II (BASIC RUN)

Fast

(ADDITIONAL STEPS)

PART III (LUMBERING WALK; REPEAT PART I TWO OCTAVES LOWER, PLAY HEAVILY
AND DELIBERATELY, AS BELOW)

Moderately slowly

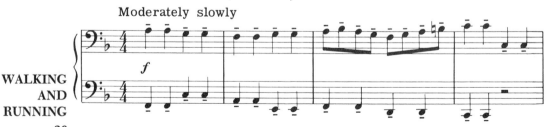

CHILDREN'S BALLET (Continued)

PART IV (TIPTOE RUN; REPEAT PART II, PLAY A LITTLE SLOWER, SOFTLY AND LIGHTLY, AS BELOW)

Moderately fast

PART V (TIPTOE WALK; REPEAT PART I, PLAY A LITTLE SLOWER, SOFTLY AND LIGHTLY, AS BELOW)

Moderately slowly

WALKING
AND
RUNNING

37

ITALIAN SAILOR'S SONG
Op. 68, No. 36

PART   I (BASIC WALK)

Robert Schumann

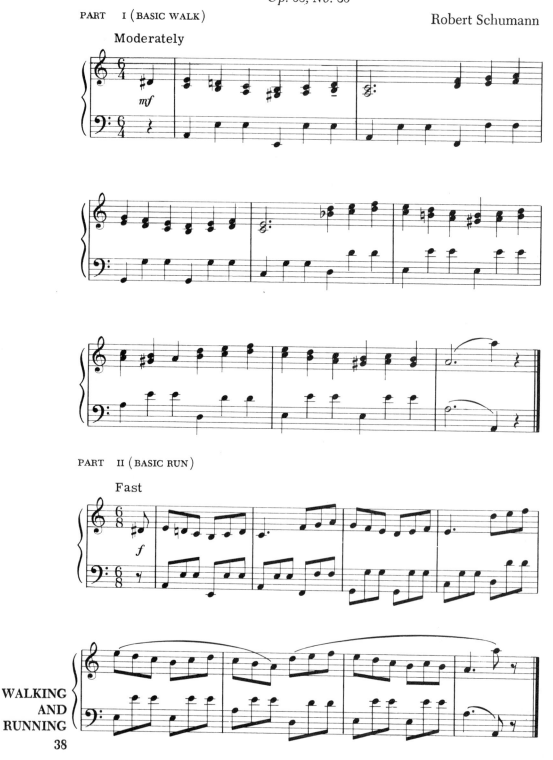

PART   II (BASIC RUN)

ITALIAN SAILOR'S SONG (Continued)

(ADDITIONAL STEPS)

PART III (HEAVY WALK; REPEAT PART I, PLAY SLOWLY AND HEAVILY, AS BELOW)

Moderately

PART IV (TIPTOE RUN; REPEAT PART II, PLAY A LITTLE SLOWER, SOFTLY AND LIGHTLY, AS BELOW)

Fast

ITALIAN SAILOR'S SONG (Continued)

PART V (LIMPING WALK; REPEAT PART I, PLAY SLIGHTLY SLOWER, IN ALTERED
RHYTHM, AS BELOW)

Moderately slowly

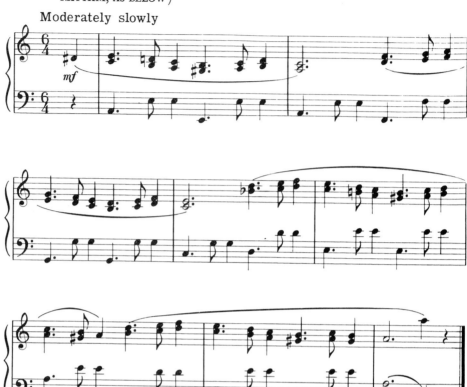

BOURRÉE

Georg Philipp Telemann

PART I (BASIC WALK)

Moderately

PART II (PEG LEGGED WALK)

Moderately

BOURRÉE (Continued)

PART III (FAST WALK; REPEAT PART I FASTER)

PART IV (LUMBERING WALK; REPEAT PART I, ADDING LOWER OCTAVE IN LEFT HAND,
PLAY SLOWLY AND HEAVILY, AS BELOW)

Slowly

PART V (FAST TIPTOE WALK; REPEAT PART I, PLAY SLIGHTLY FASTER, SOFTLY AND
LIGHTLY, AS BELOW)

Moderately fast

THE DRUM
Eugene Field

I'm a beautiful red, red drum,
And I train with soldier boys;
As up the street we come,
Wonderful is our noise,
There's Tom, and Jim, and Phil,
And Dick, and Nat, and Fred,
While Widow Cutler's Bill
And I march on ahead,
With our r-r-rat-tat-tat
And a tum-titty-um-tum-tum—
Oh, there's bushels of fun in that
For boys with a little red drum!

Poem from *Poems of Childhood* by Eugene Field, published by Charles Scribner's Sons.

7

MARCHING

Basic Marching

Motivation:
1. Play marching music. Say, "Today the drum is going to play something for you. Can you guess what it is telling you to do? Listen." (The most usual response is, "It's a parade.")
2. "Then, let's have a parade!"
3. On other days the children may take turns carrying flags, either brought from home or made during art periods.

Accompaniments: Piano, large drum, tom-tom, autoharp.

Rhythmic beat: Brisk, even, strong. Strong first beat.

Reminders:
1. Listening is silent; no movements.
2. Stop when the music stops.
3. Have a plan for the distribution of flags.

Variations in Marching

Variations in tempo and dynamics: Loud, soft; heavy, light.

Variations in direction: Backward, forward, sideward, pattern formations.

Variations in foot and arm movements: Knees raised high, on toes, swinging arms, stiff arms at side, stiff swinging arms, stiff knees, jerky.

Motivation:
1. "Today, we talked about puppets. Can you march like a puppet? I shall play while you are marching."

2. Read the poem "For a Cock."[6] Discuss the meaning of the word "strutting." Then say, "How would *you* strut?" Play a marching accompaniment as soon as some of the children start moving.
3. When the marching is finished, ask individual children to describe how this marching was different from the basic step.

Reminders:
1. Do not single out or comment upon movements while the children are in motion, for this prompts immediate imitation.
2. Comments about movements should be made only for the purpose of pointing out that there are many different ways of doing a step.
3. When discussing the movements, be sure to use vocabulary descriptive enough to avoid demonstrations.
4. Add marching to the combinations when the children respond well in this step.

Suggested Poetry for Motivation

(*See Poetry References*)
Farjeon, E., "For a Cock" (Stanza 1)[6]
John, "The Band"[4]
Miller, O. B., "The Circus Parade" (Stanzas 1 and 2)[1, 4]
Stevenson, R. L., "Marching Song"[1]

PRINCE'S MARCH

Anthony Young

MARCHING (ALSO FOR HIGH-STEPPING MARCH, PLAY STACCATO)
46

TRUMPET TUNE

(STATELY MARCH)

Henry Purcell

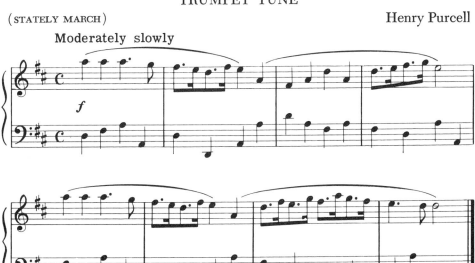

(ALSO FOR HIGH-STEPPING MARCH, PLAY STACCATO)

KING WILLIAM'S MARCH

Jeremiah Clarke

(ALSO FOR STATELY WALK, PLAY SLOWLY; FOR HIGH-STEPPING MARCH, PLAY STACCATO)

MARCHING

MARCH

Dmitri Shostakovich

Moderately

(ALSO FOR SWINGING AND SWAYING, PLAY AS SHOWN BELOW, SLOWLY; FOR SKIPPING, PLAY AS SHOWN BELOW, MODERATELY FAST)

Supplementary Music for Accompaniments

MARCHING

Music for Young Americans, Kindergarten Book[2]
    Pace, R., "Marching" (p. 102)

Music for Young Americans, Book One[3]
    Elston, R., "March" (p. 115)
    Pace, R., "On the Street" (p. 114)

Birchard Music Series, Book One[4]
    American Folk Song, "The Yellow Rose of Texas" (p. 154)
    French Folk Song, "March of the Kings" (p. 155)
    Tcherepnin, A., "March," (p. 149)

Birchard Music Series, Kindergarten Book[5]
    Burgmüller, H., "The Noble Damsel" (p. 143)
    Fucek, J., "Under the Big Top" (p. 84)
    Kabalevsky, D., "Dance" (p. 155)
    Mozart, W. A., "Step High" (p. 137)
    Prokofieff, S., "March" (p. 141)
    Sousa, J. P., "The Stars and Stripes Forever" (p. 136)

Experiences in Music for First Grade Children[7]
    Balfe, M. W., "Marching in Our Band" (p. 16)
    Delibes, L., "March" (p. 3)
    Morgan, R. V., "Here We Go" (p. 27)
    Weber, C. M. von, "March" (p. 39)

Music through the Day, Teacher's Book[8]
    Bach, J. S., "Marche" (p. 140)
    Hollaender, A., "March" (p. 139)
    Schumann, R., "Soldier's March" (p. 157)

Our Singing World, The Kindergarten Book[9]
    Anderson, C. L., "Military March" (p. 26)
    Donizetti, G., "Rataplan" (p. 139)
    Finnish, "March" (p. 27)
    Gade, N., "Christmas Tree March" (p. 85)
    Gounod, C. F., "Soldier's March" (p. 28)
    Gretchaninoff, A., "The Tin Soldiers Marching" (p. 28)
    Gurlitt, C., "March" (p. 25)
    Italian Folk Tune, "Tiptoe March" (p. 20)
    Raff, J. J., "Birthday March" (p. 72)
    Schumann, R., "Soldiers' March" (p. 130)

Our Singing World, The First Grade Book[10]
    Anderson, C. L., "March in C Major" (p. 9)
    Anderson, C. L., "March in F Major" (p. 36)
    Balfe, M. W., "A Soldier's Life" (p. 38)
    Concone, G., "Circus Parade" (p. 112)
    Donizetti, G., "March" (p. 37)
    Gade, N., "Christmas Tree March" (p. 101)
    Gounod, C. F., "Tiptoe March" (p. 14)
    Schumann, R., "Birthday March" (p. 84)
    Schumann, R., "Processional March" (p. 41)
    Souers, M., "The Band on Parade" (p. 177)

This Is Music, Book One[11]
    Traditional English Dance, "The Staines Morris Tune" (p. 184)

MARCHING

49

THE LITTLE JUMPING GIRLS
Kate Greenaway

Jump—jump—jump
   Jump away
From this town into
   The next, today.

Jump—jump—jump
   Jump over the moon;
Jump all the morning,
   And all the noon . . . .

Jump—jump—jump
   Jump far away;
And all come home
   Some other day.

Poem reprinted from *Marigold Garden/Under the Window* by Kate Greenaway with the permission of the publishers, Frederick Warne & Company.

8

JUMPING AND BOUNCING

Basic Jumping and Bouncing

Motivation:

1. "When we walk we step on one foot at a time. When we run we step on one foot at a time. When we march, how many feet do we step on at one time? Can you move using both feet at the same time? Try it." Play an accompaniment.

2. "Listen to the music. When I say, 'Go,' do what the music tells you to do." Play the rhythm in an exaggerated manner and rather fast. When the children are in motion, adjust the tempo of the music to their own pace. This method rarely fails to obtain the desired response.

3. After the movement stops, have the children name what they have been doing, and let them tell you that both feet move in unison when jumping or bouncing.

Accompaniments: Tom-tom, wood blocks, sticks, autoharp, or piano.

Rhythmic beat:

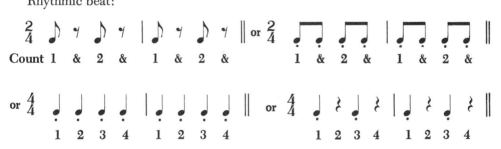

Reminders:

1. During each rhythms lesson, repeat previously acquired rhythms through the use of combined forms. (See Chapters 6 and 19.)

2. Do not refer to pieces of music as suited only to specific rhythms, such as walking music. To avoid such associations in the children's minds, use the same tune for different steps. The Index of Piano Music will facilitate finding

music that can be used in this manner. For example, Telemann's "Bourrée" can be used for walking and bouncing.

3. For jumping, play loud, heavy accompaniment. For bouncing, play the same accompaniment softer and lighter.
4. Nonpianists should play a chord (three or four keys played simultaneously) in one of the rhythmic patterns shown above.

Variations in Jumping and Bouncing

Variations in tempo, dynamics, and rhythm: Slow or fast, light or heavy, accenting one out of four.

Variations in direction: Side to side, back and forth, straight lines, zigzag, curves, backwards, all around, low and high.

Variations in leg and arm movements: One foot forward, one back; legs crossed; on all fours; arms above head; arms sideward.

Motivation:
1. "Do you know any animals that jump to move about?" Ask children who have named various animals to demonstrate their movements. Point out that each child has jumped in a different way and that all were good. Ask the other children to jump like a particular animal.
2. Repeat this procedure with several other animals.
3. Suggest bouncing like a large ball, a small ball, a soft ball.
4. Place small boxes or blocks on the floor at intervals, or in a pattern, so the children must jump in a zigzag direction.
5. Suggest jumping or bouncing to a specific distance, with a rope, or up to the ceiling.

Suggested Poetry for Motivation

(See Poetry References)
Greenaway, K., "The Little Jumping Girls"[1, 5]
Mother Goose, "Jack Be Nimble"[1, 8]
Old Rhyme, "Over in the Meadow" (Stanza 7)[6]
Watson, S. R., "Bouncing Ball"[3]

TRIO
from Minuet in F

Franz Schubert

Moderately

FOR CHILDREN
Vol. I, No. XXXII

Béla Bartók

Fast

(ALSO FOR HOPPING, PLAY MODERATELY SLOWLY AND SOFTLY, BRINGING OUT TREBLE;
FOR SLIDING, PLAY MODERATELY SLOWLY AND SMOOTHLY, WITHOUT STACCATO)

**JUMPING
AND
BOUNCING**

53

BAGATELLE

Johann Nepomuk Hummel

Moderately fast

ÉCOSSAISE IN G

Ludwig van Beethoven

Moderately fast

JUMPING AND BOUNCING (ALSO FOR HOPPING, PLAY MODERATELY SLOWLY AND SOFTLY, BRINGING OUT TREBLE; FOR BENDING AND STRETCHING, TWISTING AND TURNING, PLAY SLOWLY AND SMOOTHLY, WITHOUT STACCATO)

FIRST DANCE

Dmitri Kabalevsky

Moderately

Supplementary Music for Accompaniment

(*See Music References*)

The American Singer, Book One[1]
    Beethoven, L. van, "Sonata" (p. 111)
    Schumann, R., "The Strange Man" (p. 123)

Music for Young Americans, Kindergarten Book[2]
    Elston, R., "Theme," (p. 98)
    Pace, R., "Impromptu" (p. 104)

Music for Young Americans, Book One[3]
    Hooley, D., "Modern Age" (p. 133)
    Hooley, D., "Tom-Toms" (p. 130)
    Pace, R., "Indian Dance" (p. 131)
    Stolzfus, C., "A Lively Tune" (p. 121)
    Tchaikovsky, P. I., "Theme in D" (p. 120)

Birchard Music Series, Book One[4]
    Bartok, B., "Play" (p. 148)
    Beethoven, L. van, "Theme" (p. 172)
    Folk Tune, "Czech Dance" (p. 181)
    Haydn, F. J., "Melody" (p. 142)
    Kabalevsky, D., "Polka" (p. 156)
    Wieck, "Etude" (p. 159)

Birchard Music Series, Kindergarten Book[5]
    Bartok, B., "Dance" (p. 144)
    Burgmuller, H., "The Noble Damsel" (p. 143)
    Kabalevsky, D., "Dance" (p. 155)
    Mozart, W. A., "Step High" (p. 137)
    Prokofieff, S., "March" (p. 141)

Experiences in Music for First Grade Children[7]
    Beethoven, L. van, "Theme" (p. 128)
    Gillet, E., "The Mill" (p. 82)
    Schumann, R., "A Strange Man" (p. 42)
    Vené, R., "Catch My Doggie" (p. 14)

Music through the Day, "Teacher's Book[8]
    Corelli, A., "Gigue" (p. 132)
    Gretchaninoff, A., "Out for a Walk" (p. 131)
    Massenet, J., "Aragonaise" (p. 150)
    Schubert, F., "Ländler" (p. 134)
    Schumann, R., "Papillons" (p. 141)
    Zilcher, H., "Sleighride" (p. 136)

Our Singing World, The Kindergarten Book[9]
    Balfe, M. W., "Happy and Light" (p. 14)
    Donizetti, G., "Rataplan" (p. 139)
    Gade, N., "Christmas Tree March" (p. 85)
    Gluck, C. W., "Sicilienne" (p. 16)
    Schumann, R., "Papillons" (p. 108)
    Verdi, G., "Playing Train" (p. 132)

Our Singing World, The First Grade Book[10]

Corelli, A., "We Run" (p. 11)
Gurlitt, C., "Scherzo" (p. 147)
Moszkowski, M., "Scherzino" (p. 12)
Rubinstein, A., "Trotting Horses" (p. 23)
Swiss Folk Tune, "The Swiss Maid" (p. 15)
Weber, C. M. von, "Song of the Shepherdess" (p. 191)
Welsh Air (p. 16)

This Is Music, Book One[11]

Scotch Folk Tune, "Highland Fling" (p. 184)

THE GRASSHOPPER AND THE BIRD
James Reeves

... So the grasshopper hopped
Four hops and away
  Snick!
    Click!
      Flick!
      Slick!
Four hops and away
To the edge of the hay
Zik-a-zik zik-a-zik
For the rest of the day.

Poem from the book *The Blackbird in the Lilac* by James Reeves. Published 1959 in the U.S.A. by E. P. Dutton & Co., Inc. and in London by the Oxford University Press and reprinted with their permission.

9

HOPPING

Basic Hopping

Children hop on one foot at a time, even though they may be aware that animals hop with two feet.

Motivation:
1. Begin with a short background story such as "Last night Jimmy was racing through the house. He tripped over one of his toys and hurt his ankle. He had to go to the doctor. The doctor bandaged his ankle and told Jimmy not to use that foot to walk. Can you show me how Jimmy will walk today?"
2. Do not use accompaniment at this point.
3. Discuss the step. Have the children give you the word "hopping," and be sure they understand that it means jumping on one foot. The movement is up in the air and down.
4. Add accompaniment.

Accompaniments: Clap hands, tap stick, wood block, autoharp, piano.

Rhythmic beat: Light and fast, short and detached, or uneven long and short.

Count 1 & 2 & 1 & 2 &   1 & 2 & 3 & 1 & 2 & 3 &   1,2   & 1,2   &

Reminders:
1. Coordination is difficult in this step. Some children may have to hold one foot or may alternate feet; both are acceptable. Continually remind the group what the step is and, gradually, more children will perform it properly.
2. The children's movements will be jerky. Remember this when adding the step to the combinations.
3. Hopping tires children quickly and should be used briefly each time.
4. For additional hopping music, see the Index of Piano Music.

Variations in Hopping

Variations in direction: Hopping in place, forward and backward pattern, straight lines, curves, zigzag.

Variations in leg and arm movements: Free leg forward or back, arms straight up, arms sideward, hands on hips, hand holding leg up.

Motivation:
1. "We know the kangaroo jumps. But, some animals hop to move about. Do you know any animals that hop?" (Frogs, toads, rabbits, birds.)
2. "Can you show how the toad (or any named animal) hops?" (This is apt to be a very interesting variation with some children down on all fours.)
3. "Can you teach me how to play hopscotch?" (Children will generally move in a zigzag pattern with arms out to the sides and will usually overlook the need for a hopscotch diagram.)
4. The poem "Hippity Hop to Bed"[1, 4, 8] is good for bringing the Jimmy analogy back into the classroom. Ask to be shown how Jimmy would hippety hop to bed with his sore foot.

Suggested Poetry for Motivation

(*See Poetry References*)
Allen, M. L., "What is it?"[1]
Bennett, R. B., "Circus Day"[12]
Jackson, L. F., "Hippity Hop to Bed"[1, 4, 8]
Lear, E., "The Duck and the Kangaroo"[1, 4, 6]
Milne, A. A., "Hoppity"[1, 7, 9, 13]
Robinson, T., "Little Lady Wren"[1, 3]

FOUR LÄNDLERS, NO. I
from "Hommage aux Belles Viennoises"

Franz Schubert

(ALSO FOR JUMPING AND BOUNCING, PLAY MODERATELY FAST)

RUSSIAN FOLK SONG

Ludwig van Beethoven

(ALSO FOR TIPTOE RUN, PLAY FAST; FOR JUMPING AND BOUNCING, PLAY MODERATELY FAST, AND HEAVILY)

HOPPING

61

FOR CHILDREN
Vol. I, No. XXVI

Béla Bartók

Moderately slowly

(ALSO FOR LIMPING WALK, PLAY AT SAME SPEED, BUT BRING OUT BASS)

SCHERZINO

Johann Georg Witthauer

Moderately

HOPPING (ALSO FOR JUMPING AND BOUNCING, PLAY MODERATELY FAST)

AUSTRIAN FOLK THEME

Slowly

Carl Czerny

(ALSO FOR SLIDING, PLAY MODERATELY AND SMOOTHLY, WITHOUT STACCATO)

Supplementary Music for Accompaniment

(*See Music References*)
The American Singer, Book One[1]
　　Beethoven, L. van, "Écossaises" (p. 126)
Music for Young Americans, Kindergarten Book[2]
　　Bach, J. C., "Andante Cantabile" (p. 108)
　　Hooley, D., "Folk Theme" (p. 103)
　　Pace, R., "Rhythmic Theme in F" (p. 96)
Birchard Music Series, Book One[4]
　　Rebikov, V. I., "The Clown" (p. 168)
　　Vishkarev, "Estonian Dance" (p. 140)
Birchard Music Series, Kindergarten Book[5]
　　Danish Folk Dance, "Crested Hen" (p. 139)
　　Irish Jig, "Irish Washerwoman" (p. 140)
　　Tansman, A., "Bouncing Ball" (p. 142)
Experiences in Music for First Grade Children[7]
　　Mueller, E. A., "Hopping Frogs" (p. 65)
Music through the Day, Teacher's Book[8]
　　Delibes, L., "Passepied" (p. 158)
　　Schubert, F., "Ländler" (p. 134)
Our Singing World, The Kindergarten Book[9]
　　Gounod, C. F., "The Rabbit" (p. 19)
　　Haydn, F. J., "Allegro" (p. 151)
Our Singing World, The First Grade Book[10]
　　Gounod, C. F., "Tiptoe March" (p. 14)
　　Schubert, F., "Allegro" (p. 18)
This Is Music, Book One[11]
　　Scotch Folk Tune, "Highland Fling" (p. 184)

HOPPING

WITH OUR SLEDS
Louise Kessler

Down the hillside we are sliding,
Smooth is the snow:
Slow–ly, slow–ly climbing up–ward,
Down a–gain we go.

Lyric from *Rhythms and Rimes* of the *World of Music* series. Used by
permission of Ginn and Company, owner of the copyright.

10

SLIDING

Basic Sliding

Motivation:
1. Read poem "Icy."[3]
2. Ask "When you slide on ice, do you go on your stomach? No? Then show me how you slide."
3. Try the same movement with accompaniment.

Accompaniments: Sand blocks, ripple rhythm sticks, piano.

Rhythmic beat: One long and one short with the first beat strong, the second beat weaker (as in a waltz).

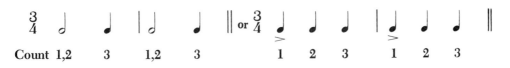

Reminders:
1. Sliding, swinging, swaying, and rocking quickly become favorites. Children need little motivation to follow their distinct rhythm. These movements can be added to earlier combinations almost immediately.
2. Be sure to have a definite swing in your accompaniment.

Variations in Sliding

Variations in direction: Sidewards, backwards, dancing with a partner, low, high, circles, curves.

Variations in tempo: Slow, fast, medium.

Motivation: Say, "Let's go skating." After the action, the children will discover that they have been sliding.

Suggested Poetry for Motivation

(*See Poetry References*)
Bacmeister, R. W., "Icy"[3]
Bush, J., "The Little Red Sled"[1]
Fyleman, R., "The Best Game the Fairies Play"[1, 3, 4]

THE MUSICAL BOX
Op. 140, No. 8

Cornelius Gurlitt

SONATINA

Muzio Clementi

SONATINA (Continued)

(ALSO FOR SWINGING, SWAYING, AND ROCKING, PLAY AS WRITTEN; FOR PUSHING AND
PULLING, PLAY SLOWLY)

PAPILLONS
Op. 2, No. 10

Robert Schumann

(ALSO FOR JUMPING AND BOUNCING, PLAY MODERATELY FAST, RATHER HEAVILY, WITH
STACCATO)

SLIDING

VALSE SERENADE

Eduard Poldini

Moderately

(ALSO FOR SWINGING, SWAYING, AND ROCKING, PLAY AS WRITTEN; FOR PUSHING AND PULLING, PLAY SLOWLY)

SLIDING

Supplementary Music for Accompaniment

(See Music References)

The American Singer, Book One[1]
    Norwegian Folk Song, "Mountain March" (p. 142)
    Schumann, R., "Sicilienne" (p. 134)
    Waldteufel, E., "Skaters' Waltz" (p. 134)

Music for Young Americans, Kindergarten Book[2]
    Hooley, D., "Waltz" (p. 96)
    Waite, F., "Waltz in E♭" (p. 106)

Music for Young Americans, Book One[3]
    Elston, R., "Waltz in D" (p. 123)
    Schubert, F., "Waltz Melody" (p. 125)
    Waite, F., "In the Orchard" (p. 123)

Birchard Music Series, Book One[4]
    German Folk Song, "The Nightingale" (p. 140)
    Rameau, J. P., "Gigue" (p. 177)

Birchard Music Series, Kindergarten Book[5]
    Austrian Folk Dance, "Tyrolean Dance" (p. 150)
    Schumann, R., "Reaper's Song" (p. 152)
    Strauss, J., "Southern Roses" (p. 151)
    Waldteufel, E., "Skaters' Waltz" (p. 149)

Experiences in Music for First Grade Children[7]
    Grieg, E., "Waltz" (p. 58)
    Morgan, R. V., "My Swing" (p. 10)

Music through the Day, Teacher's Book[8]
    Berlioz, H., "Ballet of the Sylphs" (p. 146)
    Delibes, L., "Waltz of the Doll" (p. 143)
    Dvorak, A., "Waltz" (p. 148)

Our Singing World, The Kindergarten Book[9]
    Brahms, J., "Waltz" (p. 31)
    Gurlitt, C., "Skaters' Dance" (p. 102)
    Poldini, E., "Valse Serenade" (p. 100)
    Schubert, F., "Waltz" (p. 34)
    Schumann, R., "Roller Skating" (p. 32)

Our Singing World, The First Grade Book[10]
    Borowski, F., "Valsette" (p. 140)
    Brahms J., "Waltz" (p. 139)
    Brahms, J. "Waltz No. 1" (p. 27)
    Donizetti, G., "Bouncing Balls" (p. 26)
    Fontaine, C., "Swing Song" (p. 31)
    Gounod, C. F., "Swinging" (p. 30)
    Gretchaninoff, A., "Skating" (p. 29)
    Koschat, T., "Waltz No. 5" (p. 28)
    Schubert, F., "Waltz" (p. 120)

THE SWING
Robert Louis Stevenson

How do you like to go up in a swing,
    Up in the air so blue?
Oh I do think it the pleasantest thing
    Ever a child can do!

Up in the air and over the wall,
    Till I can see so wide,
Rivers and trees and cattle and all
    Over the countryside—

Till I look down on the garden green,
    Down on the roof so brown—
Up in the air I go flying again,
    Up in the air and down!

Poem from *A Child's Garden of Verses* by Robert Louis Stevenson,
published by The World Publishing Company.

11

SWINGING, SWAYING, AND ROCKING

Basic Swinging, Swaying, and Rocking

Motivation:
1. Play an accompaniment.
2. Ask the children to guess what the music is telling them to do. (They may need help in finding the right words.)
3. Tell them to move with the accompaniment.
4. To develop large movements of arms and deep bending of legs, suggest going high up in the air in a swing.

Accompaniments: Sand blocks, large and small drum simultaneously, triangle, piano, autoharp.

Rhythmic beat: Waltz-like swinging. Accent the first beat out of every three.

Count 1,2 3 4,5 6 1,2 3 4,5 6   1,2 3 4 5 6 1,2 3 4 5 6   1,2 3 1,2 3

Reminder: Do not forget that this rhythm can be included in the combinations almost immediately.

Variations in Swinging, Swaying, and Rocking

Variations in direction: Back and forth, side to side (windshield wiper).
Variations in arm movements: Partners join hands to make a swing (this comes without suggestion), forward (carrying a heavy pail).

71

Motivation: Associate the particular movement with specifics such as rocking baby, swaying trees, animals' movements (elephant's trunk), rocking chair, a pendulum.

Reminder: For all steps, continually vary tempo and volume. This helps to achieve variations.

Suggested Poetry for Motivation

(*See Poetry References*)
Allingham, W., "A Swing Song"[6]
Colum, P., "The Ballad of Downal Baun"[2]
Farrar, J., "Broom" (Stanza 4)[4]
Richards, L. E., "The Monkeys and the Crocodile"[1, 2]
Wing, H., "A Rock-a-Bye Song"[4]

PASTORALE

Carl Philipp Emanuel Bach

SWINGING SWAYING ROCKING

(ALSO FOR SLIDING, PLAY AS WRITTEN; FOR PUSHING AND PULLING, PLAY AS WRITTEN)

BAGATELLE
Op. 33, No. 3

Moderately

Ludwig van Beethoven

(ALSO FOR SLIDING, PLAY AS WRITTEN; FOR PUSHING AND PULLING, PLAY AS WRITTEN)

CRADLE SONG

Moderately fast

Theodor Kullak

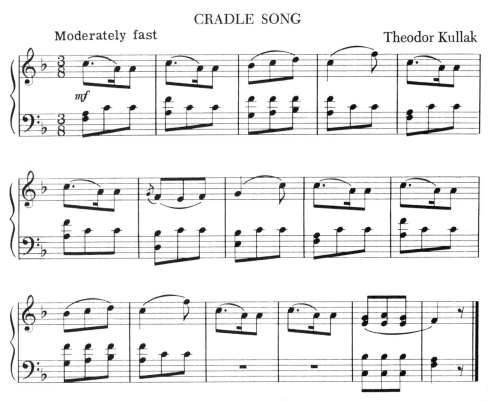

(ALSO FOR PUSHING AND PULLING, PLAY MODERATELY SLOWLY)

**SWINGING
SWAYING
ROCKING**

RONDO

Moderately fast   Wolfgang Amadeus Mozart

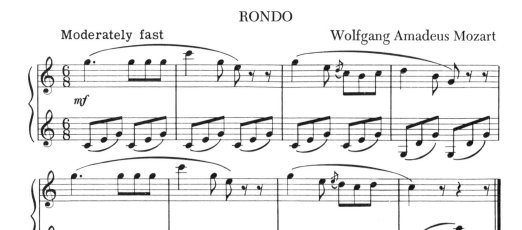

(ALSO FOR SLIDING, PLAY AS WRITTEN; FOR PUSHING AND PULLING, PLAY AS WRITTEN)

LARGHETTO
from "Three Easy Pieces on Five Notes"

Igor Stravinsky

Slowly

(ALSO FOR PUSHING AND PULLING, PLAY AS WRITTEN; FOR SKIPPING, PLAY FAST AND LIGHTLY; FOR HOPPING, PLAY MODERATELY, WITH STACCATO)

Supplementary Music for Accompaniment

SWINGING
SWAYING
ROCKING

(See Music References)
The American Singer, Book One[1]
     Brahms, J., "Waltz" (p. 143)
     Strauss, J., "The Blue Danube Waltz" (p. 145)

Music for Young Americans, Kindergarten Book[2]
    Mozart, W. A., "At a Picnic" (p. 101)
    Pace, R., "Barcarolle" (p. 95)
    Pace, R., "A Dance" (p. 104)
Music for Young Americans, Book One[3]
    Hooley, D., "Waltz in C" (p. 124)
    Mitchell, L., "On the Range" (p. 122)
    Pace, R., "Barcarolle" (p. 129)
    Pace, R., "Sicilienne" (p. 126)
Birchard Music Series, Book One[4]
    German Folk Song, "The Nightingale" (p. 140)
    Schubert, F., "Cradle Song" (p. 178)
    Strauss, J., "Waltz" (p. 176)
    Traditional Waltz, "The Primrose Ball" (p. 177)
Birchard Music Series, Kindergarten Book[5]
    Mozart, W. A., "Theme" (p. 132)
    Schumann, R., "Reaper's Song" (p. 152)
    Strauss, J., "Southern Roses" (p. 151)
    Waldteufel, E., "Skaters' Waltz" (p. 149)
Music for Early Childhood[6]
    Hiller, A., and Holty, L., "Bouncing Balls" (p. 38)
Experiences in Music for First Grade Children[7]
    Brahms, J., "Waltz" (p. 22)
    Morgan, R. V., "My Swing" (p. 10)
Music through the Day, Teacher's Book[8]
    Brahms, J., "Waltz" (p. 137)
    Delibes, L., "Waltz of the Doll" (p. 143)
    Hebrides Folk Tune, "Going to Pasture" (p. 63)
    Scottish Melody, "Arran Boat Song" (p. 142)
Our Singing World Series, The Kindergarten Book[9]
    Brahms, J., "Waltz" (p. 31)
    Delibes, L., "Valse Lente" (p. 156)
    Purcell, H., "Harvest Home" (p. 29)
    Schubert, F., "Waltz" (p. 34)
    Schumann, R., "Cradle Song" (p. 59)
    Schumann, R., "Roller Skating" (p. 32)
Our Singing World, The First Grade Book[10]
    Borowski, F., "Valsette" (p. 140)
    Donizetti, G., "Bouncing Balls" (p. 26)
    Fontaine, C., "Swing Song" (p. 31)
    Gounod, C. F., "Swinging" (p. 30)
    Gretchaninoff, A., "Skating" (p. 29)
    Koschat, T., "Waltz No. 5" (p. 28)
    Schubert, F., "Impromptu" (p. 35)
This Is Music, Book One[11]
    Schumann, R., "Little Lullaby" (p. 185)

PONY

Gretchen O. Murray

Pony, pony where can you be?
Come, gallop across the meadow to me!

Pony, pony where shall we go?
We never will tell, and no one will know.

12

GALLOPING

Basic Galloping

Motivation:
1. Say, "I'm going to play a rhythm I think you know. See if you can tell me what it makes you think of. Listen." Play the accompaniment (use tone blocks). The answer is almost always, "Horses." Then, quickly let the children be horses.
2. Elicit from the children what this movement is called.

Accompaniments: Tone blocks, rhythm sticks, piano.

Rhythmic beat: Strong, uneven, and not too fast.

$$\frac{2}{4},\frac{3}{4}, \text{or} \frac{4}{4} \quad \text{♩♩ ♩♩ ♩♩ ♩♩} \quad \| \quad \frac{6}{8},\frac{9}{8}, \text{or} \frac{12}{8} \quad \text{♩ ♪♩ ♪♩ ♪♩ ♪}\|$$

Count   1 & uh 2 & uh 3 & uh 4 & uh   1,2 3 4,5 6 7,8 9 10,11 12

Reminders:
1. Boys tend to become boisterous. When this happens, stop accompaniment and remind all the children that the music tells them how fast to go.
2. This is a difficult rhythm requiring more coordination, as in hopping and skipping. Have the children gallop only for brief intervals. Do not teach or demonstrate the step.

Variations in Galloping

Variations in tempo: Slower, faster.
Variations in dynamics: Softer, louder.

Motivation:
1. Use a poem or picture to stimulate the degree of speed and/or dynamics.
2. "How does a pony sound when he runs? Can someone play the sound on the tone block? Is it quieter or louder than a big horse? Can you trot like a pony?"

Suggested Poetry for Motivation

(*See Poetry References*)
Edey, M. and Grider, D., "Trot Along, Pony"[1, 13]
De la Mare, W., "The Huntsmen" [1, 14]
Mitchell, L. S., "If I Were a Little Pig" (stanza 2)[3]
Mother Goose, "A Farmer Went Trotting upon His Gray Mare"[1, 4]
Mother Goose, "This is the Way the Ladies Ride"[1]
Mother Goose, "To Market, to Market, To Buy a Fat Pig"[1, 8]
Unknown, "The Milkman's Horse"[3]

GIGUE À L'ANGLOISE

Georg Philipp Telemann

GALLOPING (ALSO FOR SWINGING, SWAYING, AND ROCKING, PLAY SLOWLY; FOR TWISTING AND TURNING, PLAY MODERATELY)

78

from LIGHT CAVALRY OVERTURE

Franz von Suppé

HIGHLAND SCHOTTISCHE

Scottish Folk Tune

(ALSO FOR SKIPPING, PLAY MODERATELY SLOWLY AND LIGHTLY; FOR JUMPING AND BOUNCING, PLAY MODERATELY FAST, WITH HEAVY BASS)

GALLOPING

GALLOPING
from Op. 39

Dmitri Kabalevsky

CURIOUS STORY

Stephen Heller

GALLOPING (ALSO FOR SKIPPING, PLAY MODERATELY AND LIGHTLY)

Supplementary Music for Accompaniment

(*See Music References*)
The American Singer, Book One[1]
    Reinecke, C., "Hunting Song" (p. 127)
    Schumann, R., "Wild Horseman" (p. 128)
Music for Young Americans, Kindergarten Book[2]
    Hooley, D., "Folk Theme" (p. 103)
    Pace, R., "Gigue" (p. 97)
    Pace, R., "Rhythmic Theme in F" (p. 96)
Music for Young Americans, Book One[3]
    Mitchell, L., "On the Range" (p. 122)
Birchard Music Series, Book One[4]
    Folk Dance, "Louisiana French Dance" (p. 164)
    Schumann, R., "The Wild Horseman" (p. 164)
    Scottish Folk Song, "The Campbells Are Coming" (p. 163)
Birchard Music Series, Kindergarten Book[5]
    Early American Tune, "Captain Jinks" (p. 147)
    Folk Dance, "Irish Jig" (p. 146)
Music for Early Childhood[6]
    Still, W. G., "Horse" (p. 51)
Our Singing World, The Kindergarten Book[9]
    Anderson, C. L., "Galloping Horses" (p. 52)
    Corelli, A., "Gigue" (p. 13)
    Gluck, C. W., "Sicilienne" (p. 16)
    Weber, C. M. von, "Spanish Dance" (p. 15)
Our Singing World Series, The First Grade Book[10]
    Reinecke, C, "Canzonetta" (p. 129)
This Is Music, Book One[11]
    English Tune (p. 184)

LEAPERS
Maude Pennywort

My mother says that years leap.
I've never seen a one.
But I know who the leapers *are*,
And you'll know when I'm done.
Birds leap up from off the ground,
When you scare them with a sound
Woolly lambs—of course they leap
Until they grow up into sheep.
Reindeer's frosty clattering hoofs
Leap across the Christmas roofs.
And though it is a secret
I'll share it now with you—
As well as birds and animals,
I'm a leaper, too.

13

LEAPING

Basic Leaping

Leaping may be described as running with elevation; going way up in the air.

Motivation: Christmas is a good time to introduce this step. The children have been discussing and singing songs about Santa's reindeer. Suggest moving like a reindeer.

Accompaniments: Tone blocks, rhythm sticks, piano, record. (Use two different rhythm instruments, or different surfaces, to achieve high and low pitch.)

Rhythmic beat: Uneven.

$$\frac{3}{8} \quad \text{♪ ⅞ ♪ | ♪ ⅞ ♪ | ♪ ⅞ ♪ ‖ or } \frac{2}{4} \text{ ♪ | ♩. ♪ | ♩. ♪ | ♩. ‖}$$

Count 1 2 3   1 2 3   1 2 3   & 1,2 & 1,2 & 1,2

Reminders:
1. Motivation is used only for developing new movements, either basic steps or variations. Familiar rhythmic movements need no comment; the playing of the rhythmic accompaniment should be sufficient.
2. Nonpianists: On the piano, use two keys, one in the middle range, and one high. Play them alternately, using one of the rhythmic beats given above.

Variations in Leaping

Variations in height: High (as a reindeer), low (over a small puddle), up into the air.

Variations in tempo: Fast, slow.

Motivation:
1. Play music. "Does it tell you to go high or low? higher or lower? fast or slow? faster or slower?"
2. "Leap the way the music tells you."

Reminders:
1. Variations on the basic or natural step should be created by the children. If they have been stimulated from the beginning to think in terms of moving in different ways, they will offer ideas for variations without a need for motivation.
2. Do not forget to continue building combinations. (See Chapters 6 and 19.)

Suggested Poetry for Motivation

(*See Poetry References*)
Fyleman, R., "The Fountain"[4]

ON THE BICYCLE
from "Glass Beads," Op. 123

Alexander Gretchaninov

LEAPING (ALSO FOR BENDING AND STRETCHING, PLAY SLOWLY)

WILL-O'-THE WISP
Op. 140, No. 15

Cornelius Gurlitt

Moderately fast

(ALSO FOR JUMPING AND BOUNCING, PLAY MODERATELY SLOWLY)

LEAPING

A GAY LITTLE STORY
from Op. 39

Dmitri Kabalevsky

(ALSO FOR HIGH-STEPPING MARCH, PLAY MODERATELY SLOWLY, WITH MARKED ACCENTS; FOR RUNNING, PLAY VERY FAST, WITHOUT STACCATO)

PAPILLONS
Op. 2, No. 2

Robert Schumann

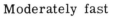

Supplementary Music for Accompaniment

(*See Music References*)
The American Singer, Book One[1]
    Gurlitt, C., "Leap for Life" (p. 124)
Music for Young Americans, Kindergarten Book[2]
    Pace, R., "Impromptu" (p. 104)
Our Singing World Series, The Kindergarten Book[9]
    Beethoven, L. van, "Presto" (p. 53)
    Gounod, C. F., "The Rabbit" (p. 19)
    Gurlitt, C., "Jumping" (p. 22)
Our Singing World Series, "The First Grade Book[10]
    Godard, B., "Postillion" (p. 22)
    Gurlitt, C., "Flying" (p. 160)
    Reinecke, C., "Canzonetta" (p. 129)
    Schytte, L., "Shadows" (p. 174)

LEAPING

SKIPPING
An American Folk Song

As I was skipping down the street,
Hi ho, hi ho, hi ho, hi ho!
A pretty girl I chanced to meet,
Hi ho, hi ho, hi ho!

Rig-a-jig-jig and away we go,
Away we go, away we go!
Rig-a-jig-jig and away we go,
Hi ho, hi ho, hi ho!

14

SKIPPING

Basic Skipping

A description of this rhythm is a walk and a hop, with alternating feet.

Motivation:
1. Tell the children to skip, and observe their action. If some say they cannot do it, ask them to try. If they are still timid, suggest they watch others. Then have the class skip together again. When the nonskippers have shown improvement, comment that more children have gotten the step.
2. After two or three different days of this, the teacher may find it necessary to demonstrate. Tell the children to watch to see what steps make a skip. If they still do not understand, skip in slow motion. (This is the only step that ever needs demonstration.)
3. With succeeding tries by the children, casually add a chant of "skip, skip, skip" interspersed with a reminder, "walk, hop, walk, hop." This greatly helps those having difficulties.

Accompaniments: The piano is best; others, such as the gourd, rattle, triangle, tambourine, and rhythm sticks can be used.

Rhythmic beat: Light, uneven, and moderately fast.

Reminders:
1. Skipping is a learned, rather than natural, response. Some children are unable to perform it by the end of the first grade.

2. It is better to accept the children's responses than to spend time drilling or suggest practicing rhythms, particularly for skipping.
3. Do not call attention to a child who has difficulty skipping.
4. When skipping is added to the combinations, it will be only for purposes of rhythm recognition. Do not expect good coordination.

Variations in Skipping

The children's own skipping has plenty of variation. They love to skip, and as coordination develops, skipping becomes easier and they become more relaxed. With increased security comes even more variation.

Suggested Poetry for Motivation

(*See Poetry References*)
Roberts, E. M., "Crescent Moon"[2]
Welles, W., "Skipping along Alone"[1]

SONATINA

Ludwig van Beethoven

(ALSO FOR SLIDING, PLAY MODERATELY SLOWLY; FOR SWINGING, SWAYING, AND ROCKING, PLAY SLOWLY)

SKIPPING

BURLESKE

Leopold Mozart

Moderately fast

SICILIENNE
Op. 68, No. 11

Robert Schumann

Moderately

(ALSO FOR SWINGING, SWAYING, AND ROCKING, PLAY SLOWLY AND SOFTLY; FOR GAL-
LOPING, PLAY FAST AND LOUD)

SKIPPING

FORLANA

Jacques Aubert

(ALSO FOR GALLOPING, PLAY MODERATELY FAST; FOR JUMPING AND BOUNCING, PLAY MODERATELY, WITH STACCATO, BRINGING OUT BASS; FOR MARCHING, PLAY MODERATELY, AS BELOW)

SKIPPING

Supplementary Music for Accompaniment

(*See Music References*)
The American Singer, Book One[1]
    Heller, S., "A Curious Story" (p. 132)
Music for Young Americans, Kindergarten Book[2]
    Hooley, D., "Folk Theme" (p. 103)
    Pace, R., "Gigue" (p. 97)
    Pace, R., "Rhythmic Theme in F" (p. 96)
Music for Young Americans, Book One[3]
    Pace, R., "On the Street" (p. 114)
Birchard Music Series, Book One[4]
    American Folk Dance, "Pop! Goes the Weasel" (p. 169)
    Kabalevsky, D., "Quick March" (p. 166)
    Louisiana French Dance, "Folk Dance" (p. 164)
Birchard Music Series, Kindergarten Book[5]
    Early American Tune, "Captain Jinks" (p. 147)
    English Folk Tune, "Country Gardens" (p. 148)
    Folk Dance, "English Dance" (p. 149)
    Irish Jig, "Irish Washerwoman" (p. 140)
    Louisiana French Folk Song, "Down in Louisiana" (p. 148)
Music for Early Childhood[6]
    French Folk Song, "Skipping Merrily" (p. 38)
Experiences in Music for First Grade Children[7]
    Norwegian Folk Song, "Christmas Carol" (p. 47)
Music through the Day, Teacher's Book[8]
    Corelli, A., "Gigue" (p. 132)
Our Singing World, The Kindergarten Book[9]
    Anderson, C. L., "Galloping Horses" (p. 52)
    Anderson, C. L., "Skip" (p. 15)
    Balfe, M. W., "Happy and Light" (p. 14)
    Corelli, A., "Gigue" (p. 13)
    English Folk Tune, "Gently My Johnny" (p. 17)
    French Folk Tune, "Dance It Merrily" (p. 17)
    Gluck, C. W., "Sicilienne" (p. 16)
    Gounod, C. F., "The Rabbit" (p. 19)
    Schumann, R., "Hunting Song" (p. 42)
Our Singing World, The First Grade Book[10]
    Anderson, C. L., "Skipping Theme" (p. 17)
    Mozart, W. A., "Theme" (p. 68)
    Schubert, F., "Allegro" (p. 18)
    Welsh Air (p. 16)
This Is Music, Book One[11]
    Traditional Nursery Tune, "To Push the Business On" (p. 185)

THE LITTLE ELF
John Kendrick Bangs

I met a little Elfman once,
Down where the lilies blow,
I asked him why he was so small,
And why he didn't grow.

He slightly frowned and with his eye
He looked me through and through—
"I'm just as big for me," said he,
"As you are big for you!"

Poem from *St. Nicholas Magazine*, Appleton-Century-Crofts, Inc.

15

BENDING AND
STRETCHING

Bending and stretching (and other movements discussed in subsequent chapters) do not have a clearly defined basic form. Every manifestation can be thought of as a variation.

Motivation: Bending and stretching are useful in developing mathematical concepts of comparison, such as, how tall, how small, how far can we reach, how wide, how narrow, squeezing into a small ball.

Examples:
1. "How tall is Jane?" (Select the tallest child.) "Is she taller than Mary? Can you make yourself as tall as Jane? taller? taller? still taller? Can you make yourself smaller? smaller? still smaller?"
2. "How many children are as tall as the flag pole?" Continue as above.
3. Begin an accompaniment as soon as the children start stretching or bending. The piano is most suitable of the instruments listed below. Play a high note for tall, a higher note for taller, and so on.

Accompaniments: Piano, autoharp—high and low strings, triangle and drum—on membrane and on side. Use two rhythm instruments for different pitches; that is, the large drum gives a low pitch (bending), the triangle gives a high pitch (stretching).

Rhythmic beat: The tempo of the rhythms as well as the extremes in pitch help to diversify and vary the movements.

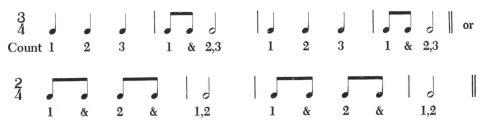

Reminder:
1. Place mats on floor. If none are available, have the children wear their smocks.

95

Suggested Poetry for Motivation

(See Poetry References)
Aldis, D., "Brooms"[3, 4]
Aldis, D., "Hiding"[1, 2, 3, 5]
Baruch, D., "Cat"[1, 2, 3, 12]
Beyer, E., "See Saw"[3]
Graham, K., "Ducks' Ditty" (Stanzas 1 and 4)[1, 2, 5, 6, 13]

LA CAROLINE

Carl Philipp Emanuel Bach

**BENDING
AND
STRETCHING**

CARNIVAL

François Couperin

Moderately fast

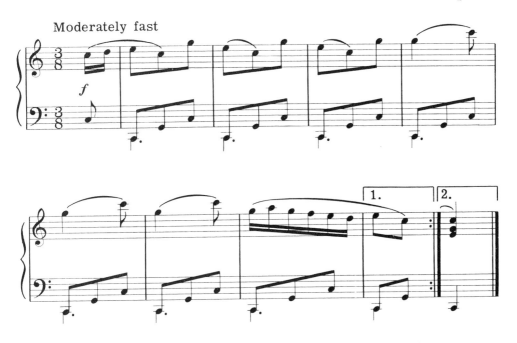

(ALSO FOR SWINGING, SWAYING, AND ROCKING, PLAY SLOWLY; FOR TWISTING AND TURNING, PLAY MODERATELY; FOR LEAPING, PLAY AS SHOWN BELOW)

Fast

BENDING AND STRETCHING

97

BAGATELLE

Ludwig van Beethoven

(ALSO FOR TWISTING AND TURNING, PLAY AS WRITTEN)

MENUETTO
from Viennese Sonatina 1

Wolfgang Amadeus Mozart

BENDING (ALSO FOR SLIDING, PLAY MODERATELY FAST)
AND
STRETCHING

Supplementary Music for Accompaniment

(*See Music References*)
Music for Young Americans, Kindergarten Book[2]
    Hooley, D., "'Little Study" (p. 99)
    Pace, R., "A Dance" (p. 104)
Music for Young Americans, Book One[3]
    Pace, R., "On the Move" (p. 117)
    Pace, R., "Sicilienne" (p. 126)
Birchard Music Series, Book One[4]
    Bashkir Folk Song, "On a Boat" (p. 138)
    MacDowell, E., "To a Water Lily" (p. 145)
    Rameau, J. P., "Gigue" (p. 177)
    Schubert, F., "Cradle Song" (p. 178)
Birchard Music Series, Kindergarten Book[5]
    Gluck, C., "Dance of the Blessed Spirits" (p. 131)
    MacDowell, E., "To a Wild Rose" (p. 132)
    Schubert, F., "Waltz" (p. 151)
    Schumann, R., "Reaper's Song" (p. 152)
Experiences in Music for First Grade Children[7]
    Mueller, E. A., "The Moon Goes by My Window" (p. 134)
Music through the Day, Teacher's Book[8]
    Delibes, L., "Waltz of the Doll" (p. 143)
    Planquette, R., "Legend of the Bells," (p. 144)
    Rebikoff, V., "A Little Girl Rocking Her Doll" (p. 154)
    Schubert, F., "Theme" from "Rosamunde" (p. 152)
Our Singing World, The Kindergarten Book[9]
    Gurlitt, C., "Skater's Dance" (p. 102)
    Iljinsky, A., "Lullaby" (p. 61)
    Karganoff, C., "Nature's Dream" (p. 104)
    Schumann, R., "Roller Skating" (p. 32)
Our Singing World, The First Grade Book[10]
    Borowski, F., "Valsette" (p. 140)
    Brahms, J., "Waltz No. 1" (p. 27)
    Fontaine, C., "Swing Song" (p. 31)
    Schubert, F., "Impromptu" (p. 35)
    Schubert, F., "Waltz" (p. 120)
    Tchaikovsky, P. I., "Mama" (p. 56)
This Is Music, Book One[11]
    Old Sea Chantey, "Skye Boat Song" (p. 185)

BENDING
AND
STRETCHING
99

MY GARDEN
Ethel H. Tewksbury

With a spade and rake and hoe,
To my garden I will go;
It is ready for me to sow
Whatever I like best.
Seeds are planted in a row,
Soon they will begin to grow;
Work! or maybe you'll never know
How nice it is to rest.

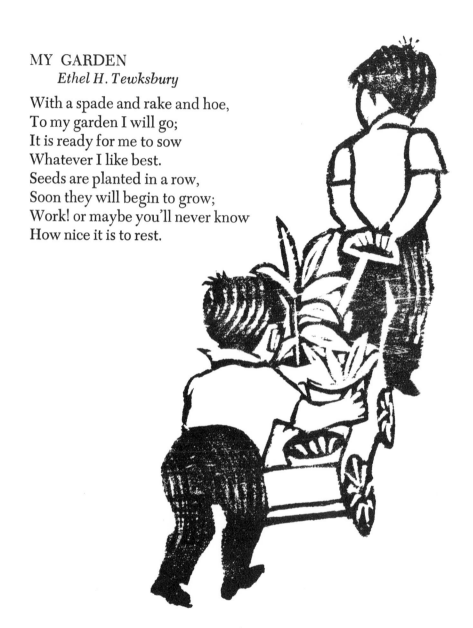

Lyric from *Rhythms and Rimes* of the *World of Music* series. Used by permission of Ginn and Company, owner of the copyright.

16

PUSHING AND PULLING

These movements include those of bending and stretching.

Motivation:
1. Read poem "Ferry Me across the Water."[2, 6] Ask, "How does the boatman ferry you across the water?" Play a rhythmic accompaniment while the children are rowing.
2. Ask what movements they have used and what parts of the body are involved.
3. Ask what else they can do with the same body movements. Some suggestions will be: pushing a baby in a carriage, pushing a wheelbarrow, pushing an automobile stuck in the snow (with shoulders, hands, feet, knees, whole body), pulling a sled up a hill, pulling a wagon, pulling on a rope (tug of war).

Accompaniments: Sand blocks, wood blocks, tone blocks, piano.

Rhythmic beat: Uneven; in a leisurely manner.

Reminder:
1. Rhythms need not always be part of a formal period. There are many times during the day when motivation is naturally supplied by the children. During free play time or in connection with science activities, these movements are carried on through dramatic play and experimentation. Take advantage of such opportunities as they arise.

Example: The children are playing house. While one is pushing the doll carriage, comment, "You are pushing and pulling." Or, ask the children to tell you what movements are being made. Then, "I'm going to see if I can play what you are doing." Play an accompaniment. Ask, "Do you think the accompaniment moves like you did?"

Suggested Poetry for Motivation

(See Poetry References)
Baruch, D., "Lawn-mower"[2, 3, 12]
Fyleman, R., "Very Lovely" (Stanza 1)[1, 3, 4]
Rosetti, C., "Ferry Me across the Water"[2, 6]
Tippett, J. S., "Tugs"[4]

SARABANDE

Johann Jakob de Neufville

PUSHING AND PULLING (ALSO FOR SWINGING, SWAYING, AND ROCKING, PLAY MODERATELY)

102

FOR CHILDREN
Vol. II, No. XVII

Béla Bartók

(ALSO FOR SWINGING, SWAYING, AND ROCKING, PLAY SLOWLY AND QUIETLY)

SONG FROM THE CREUSE

César Franck

BOATING
Op. 96, No. 4

Albert Löschhorn

Supplementary Music for Accompaniment

(*See Music References*)
Music for Young Americans, Kindergarten Book[2]
    Pace, R., "Barcarolle" (p. 95)
    Pace, R., "A Dance" (p. 104)
Music for Young Americans, Book One[3]
    Bach, J. C., "Romanza" (p. 128)
    Pace, R., "Barcarolle" (p. 129)
    Pace, R., "Sicilienne" (p. 126)
Birchard Music Series, Kindergarten Book[5]
    Mozart, W. A., "Theme" (p. 132)
    Strauss, J., "Southern Roses" (p. 151)
Music through the Day, Teacher's Book[8]
    Berlioz, H., "Ballet of the Sylphs" (p. 146)
    Scottish Melody, "Arran Boat Song" (p. 142)
Our Singing World Series, The Kindergarten Book[9]
    English Folk Tune, "Gently My Johnny" (p. 17)
    Poldini, E., "Valse Serenade" (p. 100)
    Purcell, H., "Harvest Home" (p. 29)
    Schumann, R., "Cradle Song" (p. 59)
Our Singing World, The First Grade Book[10]
    Brahms, J., "Waltz" (p. 139)
    Donizetti, G., "Bouncing Balls" (p. 26)
    Fontaine, C., "Swing Song" (p. 31)
    Gretchaninoff, A., "Skating" (p. 29)
    Gurlitt, C., "Easter Sunday" (p. 110)
    Schubert, F., "The Miller's Flowers" (p. 25)
    Tchaikovsky, P. I., "A Winter Morning" (p. 136)

A CHILD'S DAY
Walter de la Mare

Softly, drowsily,
Out of sleep,
Into the world again
Ann's eyes peep;

Up comes her round little
Tousled head;
And out she tumbles
From her warm bed.

Poem from *A Child's Day* by Walter de la Mare, reprinted with the permission of the Literary Trustees of Walter de la Mare and The Society of Authors.

17

TUMBLING

Motivation:
1. "Can you make yourself round like the sun? What can you do if you are round?"
2. Discuss the rolling motion: bundles of leaves rolling over the ground, barrels, hoops, dogs or cats playing, tumbling tricks of a clown. Use any one or several of these. Play an accompaniment and let the children respond naturally.

Accompaniments: Drum (use two surfaces), tambourine, gourds, piano.

Rhythmic beat: Fast, even.

Reminders:
1. Place mats on the floor, or have the children wear their smocks.
2. Variations in tumbling are a result of the individuals' natural movements and the rhythm of the accompaniment.
3. Do not forget to use this step in combinations.

Suggested Poetry for Motivation

(*See Poetry References*)
Fisher, A., "Somersaults"[3]
Milne, A. A., "Round About"[8]
Mother Goose, "Jack and Jill Went up the Hill"[1]
Richards, L. E., "Jippy and Jimmy" (Stanza 1)[1, 5]

FÜR ELISE

Ludwig van Beethoven

SONATINA

Jakob Schmitt

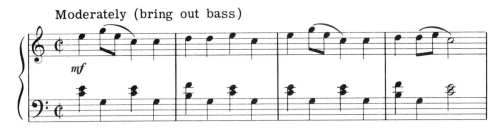

TUMBLING (ALSO FOR TIPTOE WALK, PLAY SLOWLY, WITH STACCATO)

RONDINO

Jean Philippe Rameau

(ALSO FOR TWISTING AND TURNING, PLAY SLOWLY; FOR SKIPPING, PLAY MODERATELY,
AS INDICATED BELOW)

TUMBLING
109

MINIATURE RONDO

Daniel Gottlob Türk

Supplementary Music for Accompaniment

(*See Music References*)
Birchard Music Series, Kindergarten Book[5]
    Tcherepnin, A., "Relays" (p. 152)
Experiences in Music for First Grade Children[7]
    Mueller, E. A., "The Brook" (p. 131)
Music through the Day, Teacher's Book[8]
    Bartok, B., "Round Dance" (p. 135)
    Couperin, F., "The Little Windmills" (p. 156)
    Kabalevsky, D., "A Little Joke" (p. 138)
    Massenet, J., "Aragonaise" (p. 150)
    Prokofieff, S., "Tarantelle" (p. 132)

RING-A-RING
Kate Greenaway

Ring-a-ring of little boys,
   Ring-a-ring of girls;
All around—all around,
   Twists and twirls.

You are merry children,
   "Yes, we are."
Where do you come from?
   "Not very far.

"We live in the mountain,
   We live in the tree;
And I live in the river bed
   And you won't catch me!"

Poem reprinted from *Marigold Garden/Under the Window* by Kate Greenaway with the permission of the publishers, Frederick Warne & Company.

18

TWISTING AND
TURNING

The whole body should be used in these rhythms.

Motivation:
1. Twisting and turning can fit into a science lesson on wheels or machines, or a lesson on food.
2. The egg beater is a machine. Leave one to be discovered in the science corner. When interest in its action develops, play an accompaniment while a child operates it. Then, let one turn the egg beater as accompaniment while others "are" egg beaters with their bodies.
3. Offer the class other examples, such as twisting like a snake, a monkey's tail, a piece of string dropping, a pretzel, turning like a top, a wheel.

Accompaniments: Egg beater, clacking stick across the spokes of a wheel, ripple rhythm sticks, piano.

Rhythmic beat: Several slow, even; then several faster beats.

Count 1   2   3 &   1   2   3 &   1   2   3 & 4 &   1   2   3 & 4 &

Reminder:
1. The briefer the motivation for any movement, the better. Too much talking and discussion hinders the spontaneity of response and causes the children to become dependent upon suggestions.

Suggested Poetry for Motivation

(*See Poetry References*)
Cleveland, E. L., "Snowflakes" (Stanzas 1 and 2)[3]
Sherman, F. D., "Spinning Top"[4, 12]
Unknown, "The Whirl and Twirl"[3]
Unknown, "Winter"[4]

LITTLE STUDY
Op. 68, No. 14

Robert Schumann

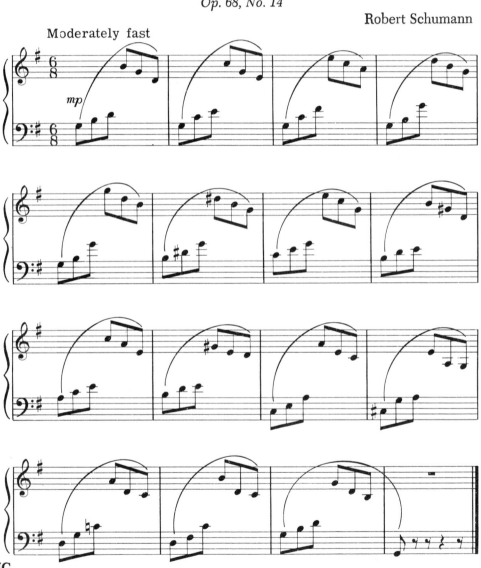

TWISTING AND TURNING

114

(ALSO FOR BENDING AND STRETCHING, PLAY SLOWLY; FOR TUMBLING, PLAY FAST)

GERMAN DANCE

Ludwig van Beethoven

(ALSO FOR TUMBLING, PLAY FAST; FOR SKIPPING, PLAY MODERATELY AND LIGHTLY, AS INDICATED BELOW)

COUNTRY DANCE

Ludwig van Beethoven

(ALSO FOR TUMBLING, PLAY FAST; FOR SKIPPING, PLAY MODERATELY SLOWLY, AS BELOW; FOR GALLOPING, PLAY FAST, AS BELOW)

MINUET

Johann Sebastian Bach

Moderately

(ALSO FOR BENDING AND STRETCHING, PLAY AS WRITTEN; FOR TUMBLING, PLAY FAST)

Supplementary Music for Accompaniment

(*See Music References*)
The American Singer, Book One[1]
    Mendelssohn, F., "Tarantella" (p. 146)
    Schumann, R., "Reaper's Song" (p. 149)

Music for Young Americans, Kindergarten Book[2]
    Kabalevsky, D., "A Fairy Tale" (p. 108)
    Schubert, F., "Écossaise" (p. 106)
Music for Young Americans, Book One[3]
    Bach, J. C., "Romanza" (p. 128)
    Pace, R., "On the Move" (p. 117)
    Pace, R., "Sicilienne" (p. 126)
Birchard Music Series, Book One[4]
    Kabalevsky, D., "Running Along" (p. 160)
    Schumann, R., "Humming Song" (p. 133)
    Zhilinsky, "Happy Children" (p. 182)
Birchard Music Series, Kindergarten Book[5]
    Bartok, B., "Folk Song" (p. 133)
    Schumann, R., "Reaper's Song" (p. 152)
Experiences in Music for First Grade Children[7]
    Beethoven, L. van, "Country Dance" (p. 85)
    Mendelssohn, F., "Presto" (p. 63)
Music through the Day, Teacher's Book[8]
    Grieg, E., "Puck" (p. 145)
    Mendelssohn, F., "Theme" from "Kinderstücke" (p. 136)
    Planquette, R., "Legend of the Bells" (p. 144)
Our Singing World, The Kindergarten Book[9]
    Grieg, E., "Birdling" (p. 107)
Our Singing World, The First Grade Book[10]
    Gluck, C. W., "Gavotte" (p. 21)
    Gretchaninoff, A., "Snowflake Dance" (p. 136)
    Heller, S., "Petite Tarantelle" (p. 33)
    Hollaender, A., "Birds in the Woods" (p. 138)
    Mendelssohn, F., "Planes and Trains" (p. 193)
    Schumann, R., "The Little Breeze" (p. 122)

THE SALT AND PEPPER DANCE
Wymond Garthwaite

One day, or no, one night—
It just happened by chance
The Salt and Pepper pots
Decided they should dance.

They skipped and skipped about
As merry as could be,
For Salt and Pepper pots
So seldom dance, you see.

They jigged and jumped and jogged—
They really did too much—
The pepper sprinkled out
And made them sneeze "Ker-Snutch!"

"Ker-Wish! Ker-Wash! Ker-Chow!"
The dancers now were through.
"We'll have to stop," they said,
"We'll have to st—Ker-Choo!"

19

COMBINING
THE RHYTHMS

As noted in Chapter 6, when children are secure in a movement, it should be used in combination with preceding steps. Thus, the children develop an ability to respond to sound through discriminative listening. For example, by the time the jumping movement is reached, the children have developed the ability to follow changes from walking to running to marching in any order or combination without being told in advance of rhythmic changes. When they are able to jump at the given tempo, jumping is then added to the combination.

As a consequence, by the end of the year, the rhythms period will consist mainly of combinations of rhythms. These may take the form of several basic steps, any basic step and some of its variations, or several basic steps and their variations. Though these rhythmic patterns are set by the teacher, it does not follow that the children will do the steps she has in mind. For example, the teacher may be playing a rhythm for sliding. Some children may hear it that way, but some may respond by sitting on the floor and rowing a boat; others may respond by rocking. All of these are good because they fit the same rhythmic pattern, and particularly because original response has been the ultimate goal.

Basically, then, the teacher presents varieties of rhythmic combinations, and the children respond with even greater variety.

The music throughout this book should be used in such a way that the children will not associate a particular tune with a rhythm, such as walking music. References of this sort must be avoided.

To achieve combination patterns, two types of musical examples are included. In one type, a simple tune is given for a specific step, then the same tune is repeated with changes in rhythm, tempo, or dynamics to achieve other steps; for example, Telemann's "Bourrée" and Haydn's "Rondo."

A good portion of the music elsewhere in the book can be treated similarly. Suggestions are given under the individual pieces of music. The Index of Piano Music lists all such music, together with the suggested combinations of rhythms, under the heading "Combinations." The "Theme and Variations" form in classical music can often be used for combinations of rhythms; for example, Corrette's "La Confession" and Mozart's "Theme and Variations." Music like this should be played without pause or comment to the children when rhythms or tempos change.

The second type of musical example is one that inherently contains rhythmic changes within the framework of a single piece of music. Such pieces are more difficult to respond to. Therefore, they should be left until the end of the school year. When they are used, prepare the children by playing the music first, while they listen for the quick changes. Heller's "Avalanche" and Haydn's "Andantino" are examples of this type given in this chapter. Additional examples are referred to under "Supplementary Music for Accompaniment."

To aid the nonpianist in formulating combinations, the Index of Basic Rhythmic Patterns has been provided in the back of the book. This will enable the teacher to find the individual patterns to be used in any desired combination of two or more rhythms. Varying the means of accompaniment (clapping hands, sticks on floor, rhythm instruments), tempo, volume, and accent, will help the children make the finer discrimination necessary to change their rhythmic responses.

In any learning situation a high degree of interest helps achieve maximum results and offsets the problems of boredom and discipline. As in other fields, children should be made aware of purposes or goals during the rhythms period. For example, "While you are walking, try to make a pattern; four steps forward and four steps backward." Or, "Try to add some other step. Can you walk and kick or walk and jump?" Such suggestions encourage more experimentation and give continued stimulation.

Since patterns and combinations are unlimited in scope, there should be no reason for lack of interest.

BOURRÉE

PART I (BASIC WALK)   Georg Philipp Telemann

Moderately

BOURRÉE (Continued)

PART II (BASIC RUN)

Fast

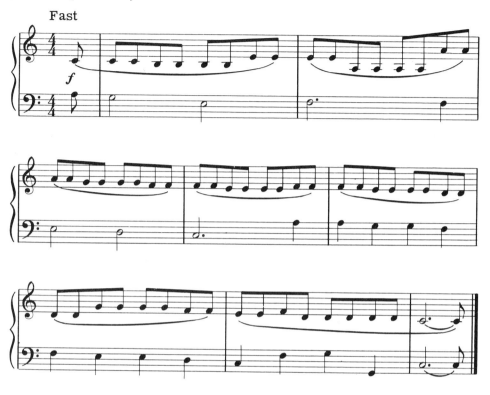

PART III (SWINGING, SWAYING, ROCKING)

Moderately fast

**COMBINING
RHYTHMS**

BOURRÉE (Continued)

PART IV (LEAPING)

Moderately

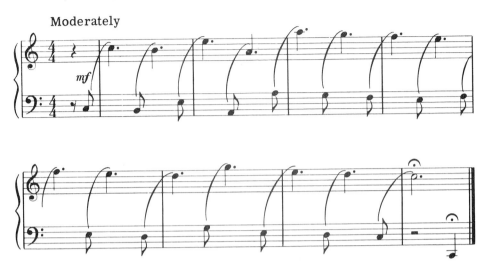

PART V (MARCHING)

Moderately, in strict time

BOURRÉE (Continued)

PART VI (GALLOPING)

Fast

PART VII (JUMPING, BOUNCING)

Moderately slowly

RONDO

PART I (WALKING)

Franz Joseph Haydn

Moderately

PART II (SKIPPING OR GALLOPING)

Moderately fast

RONDO (Continued)

PART III (SWINGING, SWAYING, ROCKING)

Slowly

PART IV (RUNNING)

Moderately fast

PART V (TWISTING, TURNING)

Moderately slowly

COMBINING RHYTHMS

RONDO (Continued)

(ADDITIONAL STEPS)
PART VI (TIPTOE RUN; PLAY PART IV LIGHTLY, A LITTLE SLOWER, AS BELOW)

Moderately

PART VII (TIPTOE WALK; PLAY PART I LIGHTLY, A LTTLE SLOWER, AS BELOW)

Moderately slowly

THEME AND VARIATIONS
K. 265

PART I (BASIC WALK)

Wolfgang Amadeus Mozart

Moderately

PART II (BASIC RUN)

Moderately fast

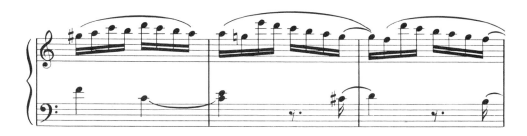

THEME AND VARIATIONS (Continued)

PART III (LIMPING WALK)

Moderately slowly

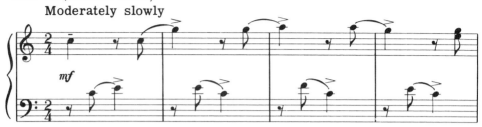

PART IV (TUMBLING OR TWISTING AND TURNING; REPEAT PART II, SLIGHTLY FASTER)

PART V (TIPTOE WALK; REPEAT PART I, SOFTLY AND LIGHTLY, AS BELOW)

Moderately

PART VI (HOPPING; REPEAT PART III, WITH STACCATO AND UNIFORM EMPHASIS, AS BELOW)

Moderately fast

LA CONFESSION

PART I (BASIC WALK)

Michel Corrette

Moderately

PART II (HIGH-STEPPING RUN)

Moderately fast

LA CONFESSION (Continued)

PART III (GALLOPING)

Fast

ANDANTINO

(BOUNCING, TURNING)

Franz Joseph Haydn

(BOUNCE) (TURN) (BOUNCE) (TURN)

Moderately

(BOUNCE) (BOUNCE)

**COMBINING
RHYTHMS**

AVALANCHE

(RUNNING, LEAPING, JUMPING)

Stephen Heller

(RUN)　　(LEAP)　　(RUN)　　(LEAP)

Fast

(JUMP)

Slower and deliberately

Supplementary Music for Accompaniment

(*See Music References*)
The American Singer, Book One[1]
　　Beethoven, L. van, "Bagatelle" (p. 123)
　　Poldini, E., "Dancing Doll" (p. 148)

Music for Young Americans, Kindergarten Book[2]
    Beethoven, L. van, "Country Dance" (p. 107)
Music for Young Americans, Book One[3]
    Hooley, D., "Tom-Toms" (p. 130)
    Pace, R., "Indian Dance" (p. 131)
    Riccio, M., "Starlight" (p. 131)
    Scott, S., "Out of Doors" (p. 119)
Birchard Music Series, Book One[4]
    Circassian Folk Dance, "Dance" (p. 147)
    Erb, M. E., "The Chime Clock" (p. 172)
    Mozart, W. A., "Allegretto" (p. 141)
Music for Early Childhood[6]
    Baldwin, L., "The Dance" (p. 61)
Experiences in Music for First Grade Children[7]
    Morgan, R. V., "At the Circus" (p. 86)
Music through the Day, Teacher's Book[8]
    Moszkowski, M., "Sparks" (p. 147)
Our Singing World Series, The Kindergarten Book[9]
    Grieg, E., "Birdling" (p. 107)
Our Singing World, The First Grade Book[10]
    Schubert, F., "Fairies" (p. 201)

Poetry References

Collections

1. Arbuthnot, May Hill, ed., *Time for Poetry: A Teacher's Anthology*. Chicago: Scott, Foresman and Company, 1951.
2. Association for Childhood Education, *Sung under the Silver Umbrella*. New York: The Macmillan Company, 1956.
3. Geismer, Barbara Peck, and Suter, Antoinette Brown, *Very Young Verses*. Boston: Houghton Mifflin Company, 1945.
4. Hubbard, Alice, and Babbitt, Adeline, eds., *The Golden Flute: An Anthology of Poetry for Young Children*. New York: The John Day Company, Inc., 1932.
5. Huffard, Grace Thompson, and Carlisle, Laura Mae, *My Poetry Book*. New York: Holt, Rinehart and Winston, Inc., 1956.
6. Love, Katherine, ed., *A Pocketful of Rhymes*. New York: Thomas Y. Crowell Company, 1946.

Individual Poets

7. Milne, A. A., *When We Were Very Young*. New York: E. P. Dutton & Co., Inc., 1924.

Music Books

8. Beattie, John W., and others, *The American Singer: Book One*, Second Edition. New York: American Book Company, 1954.
9. Grentzer, Rose Marie, and Hood, Marguerite V., *Birchard Music Series: Kindergarten Book*. Evanston, Ill.: Summy-Birchard Publishing Company, 1958.
10. Mursell, James, and others, *Music for Living Series: Music through the Day, Teacher's Book*. Morristown, N. J.: Silver Burdett Company, 1962.
11. Mursell, James, and others, *Music for Living Series: Music in Our Town, Teacher's Book*. Morristown, N. J.: Silver Burdett Company, 1962.

12. Pitts, Lilla Belle, and others, *Our Singing World Series: The First Grade Book*, Enlarged Edition. Boston: Ginn & Company, 1959.
13. Wolfe, Irving, and others, *Together We Sing Series: Music Round the Clock*, Revised Edition. Chicago: Follett Publishing Co., 1959.
14. Wolfe, Irving, and others, *Together We Sing Series: Music Round the Town*, Revised Edition. Chicago: Follett Publishing Co., 1959.

Music References

Books Containing Supplementary Music for Accompaniment

1. Beattie, John W., and others, *The American Singer: Book One*, Second Edition. New York: American Book Company, 1961.
2. Berg, Richard C., and others, *Music for Young Americans, Kindergarten Book*. New York: American Book Company, 1959.
3. Berg, Richard C., and others, *Music for Young Americans, Book One*. New York: American Book Company, 1959.
4. Ernst, Karl, and others, *Birchard Music Series: Book One*. Evanston, Ill.: Summy-Birchard Publishing Company, 1962.
5. Grentzer, Rose Marie and Hood, Marguerite V., *Birchard Music Series: Kindergarten Book*. Evanston, Ill.: Summy-Birchard Publishing Company, 1958.
6. McConathy, Osbourne, and others, *New Music Horizons Series: Music for Early Childhood*. Morristown, N. J.: Silver Burdett Company, 1952.
7. McConathy, Osbourne, and others, *New Music Horizons Series: Experiences in Music for First Grade Children*. Morristown, N. J.: Silver Burdett Company, 1949.
8. Mursell, James, and others, *Music for Living Series: Music through the Day, Teacher's Book*. Morristown, N. J.: Silver Burdett Company, 1962.
9. Pitts, Lilla Belle, and others, *Our Singing World Series: The Kindergarten Book*, Enlarged Edition. Boston: Ginn & Company, 1959.
10. Pitts, Lilla Belle, and others, *Our Singing World Series: The First Grade Book*, Enlarged Edition. Boston: Ginn & Company, 1959.
11. Sur, William R., and others, *This Is Music Series: Book One*. Boston: Allyn and Bacon, Inc., 1962.

Bibliography

Andrews, Gladys, *Creative Rhythmic Movement for Children.* Englewood Cliffs, N. J.: Prentice-Hall, Inc., 1954.

Association for Childhood Education, *Music for Children's Living.* Washington, D.C.: A.C.E.I., 1948

Byer, Maude Gerrior, *Music Education in Elementary School.* San Francisco, Calif.: Fearon Publishers, 1957.

Christianson, Helen, "Bodily Rhythmic Movements of Young Children in Relation to Rhythm in Music." New York: Bureau of Publications, Teachers College, Columbia University, 1939.

Culkin, Mabel Louise, *Teaching the Youngest.* New York: The MacMillan Company, 1950.

Ellison, Alfred, *Music with Children.* New York: McGraw-Hill Book Company, 1959.

Geri, Frank H., *Illustrated Games and Rhythms for Children.* Englewood Cliffs, N. J.: Prentice-Hall, Inc., 1955.

Hood, Marguerite V., and Schultz, E. J., *Learning Music through Rhythm.* Boston: Ginn & Company, 1949.

Hughes, Langston, *The First Book of Rhythms.* New York: Franklin Watts, Inc., 1954.

Landeck, Beatrice, *Children and Music.* New York: William Sloane Associates, 1952.

La Salle, Dorothy, *Rhythms and Dances for Elementary Schools.* New York: The Ronald Press Company, 1951.

Levy, D. M., "On the Problem of Movement Restraint, Ties, Stereotyped Movements, Hyperactivity." New York: American Journal of Orthopsychiatry, No. 14, 1944, pp. 644–670.

Mursell, James L., *Music and the Classroom Teacher.* Morristown, N. J.: Silver Burdett Company, 1951.

Newman, Theresa, *A Child and Rhythm.* New York: M. S. Mills Co., Inc., 1955.

Perham, Beatrice, *Growing up with Music*. Chicago: Neil A. Kjos Music Co., 1939.

Pitts, Lilla Belle, *The Music Curriculum in a Changing World*. Morristown, N. J.: Silver Burdett Company, 1944.

Sehon, E. L., and O'Brien, E. L., *Rhythms in Elementary Education*. New York: The Ronald Press Company, 1951.

Shafer, Mary S., *Rhythms for Children*. New York: A. S. Barnes and Company, Inc., 1938.

Sheehy, Emma Dickson, *Children Discover Music and Dance*. New York: Holt, Rinehart and Winston, Inc., 1959.

Sheehy, Emma Dickson, *The Fives and Sixes Go to School*. New York: Holt, Rinehart and Winston, Inc., 1954.

Sheehy, Emma Dickson, "Music and the Classroom Teacher." Washington, D. C.: Music Educators Journal, September–October 1950, pp. 36–37.

Sheehy, Emma Dickson, *There's Music in Children*. New York: Holt, Rinehart and Winston, Inc., 1952.

Snyder, Alice M., *Creating Music with Children*. New York: Mills Music, Inc., 1957.

Sullivan, Bernice Withers, "Rhythmic Activities in an Integrated Primary Program." Ann Arbor, Mich.: University of Michigan, Master's Thesis, February 1941.

Sutton, Rhoda R., *Creative Rhythms*. New York: A. S. Barnes and Company, Inc., 1941.

Timmerman, Maurine, *Let's Teach Music in the Elementary School*. Evanston, Ill.: Summy-Birchard Publishing Co., 1958.

Timmerman, Maurine, *Let's Make Music*. Evanston, Ill.: Summy-Birchard Publishing Co., 1958.

Veatch, Jeannette, "An Experimental Study of the Relation of a Program of Specific Creative Activities to Group Acceptance, Emotional Needs and Academic Achievement." New York: New York University, Ph.D. Final Document, 1953.

Zerbes, Laura, *Spurs to Creative Teaching*. New York: G. P. Putnam's Sons, 1959.

Indexes

Basic Rhythmic Patterns

(For Use with Rhythm Instruments)

Walking

Running

Walking and Running

Marching

Jumping and Bouncing

Hopping

Count 1 & 2 & 1 & 2 &   1 & 2 & 3 & 1 & 2 & 3 &   1,2 & 1,2 &

Sliding

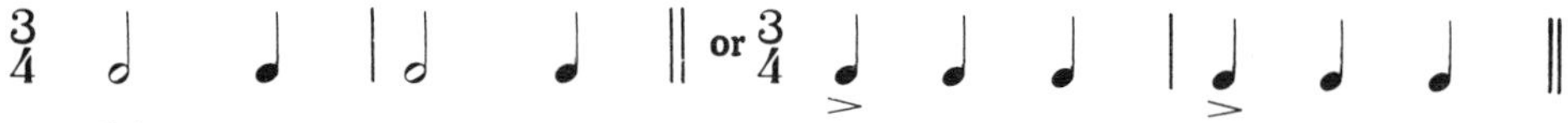

Count 1,2 3 1,2 3   1 2 3 1 2 3

Swinging, Swaying, and Rocking

Count 1,2 3 4,5 6 1,2 3 4,5 6   1,2 3 4 5 6 1,2 3 4 5 6   1,2 3 1,2 3

Galloping

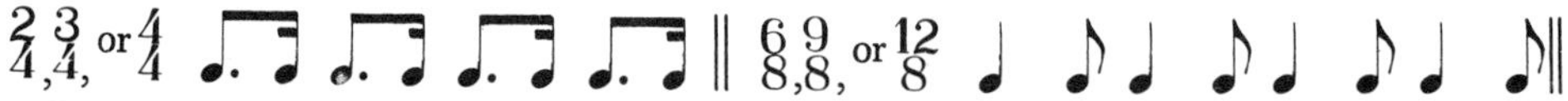

Count 1 & uh 2 & uh 3 & uh 4 & uh   1,2 3 4,5 6 7,8 9 10,11 12

Leaping

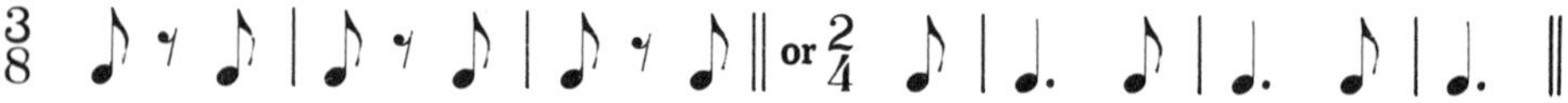

Count 1 2 3 1 2 3 1 2 3   & 1,2 & 1,2 & 1,2

Skipping

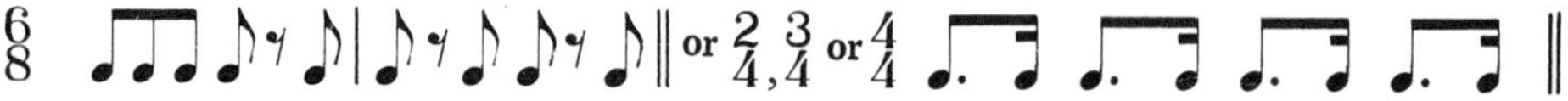

Count 1 2 3 4 5 6 1 2 3 4 5 6   1 & uh 2 & uh 3 & uh 4 & uh

or 6/8, 9/8, or 12/8

1,2 3 4,5 6 7,8 9 10,11 12

Bending and Stretching

Count 1 2 3 1 & 2,3 1 2 3 1 & 2,3 or

1 & 2 & 1,2 1 & 2 & 1,2

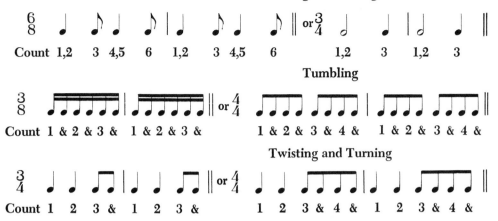

Pushing and Pulling

Count 1,2   3   4,5   6   1,2   3   4,5   6   1,2   3   1,2   3

Tumbling

Count 1 & 2 & 3 &   1 & 2 & 3 &   1 & 2 & 3 & 4 &   1 & 2 & 3 & 4 &

Twisting and Turning

Count 1   2   3 &   1   2   3 &   1   2   3 & 4 &   1   2   3 & 4 &

Piano Music

Walking

Running

Walking and Running Combinations

Marching

Jumping and Bouncing

Hopping

Sliding

Additional Selections

Swinging, Swaying, and Rocking

Selections in Chapter 11

Additional Selections

Galloping

Selections in Chapter 12

Leaping

Skipping

Bending and Stretching

Pushing and Pulling

Tumbling

Twisting and Turning

Combinations

Poetry